Decoding Revelation

John Zavicar III

NEW HARBOR PRESS
RAPID CITY, SD

Copyright © 2023 by John Zavicar III.

All rights reserved. No part of this publication may be reproduced, distributed or transmitted in any form or by any means, including photocopying, recording, or other electronic or mechanical methods, without the prior written permission of the publisher, except in the case of brief quotations embodied in critical reviews and certain other noncommercial uses permitted by copyright law. For permission requests, write to the publisher, addressed "Attention: Permissions Coordinator," at the address below

Zavicar/New Harbor Press
1601 Mt. Rushmore Rd, Ste 3288
Rapid City, SD 57701
www.NewHarborPress.com

Ordering Information:
Quantity sales. Special discounts are available on quantity purchases by corporations, associations, and others. For details, contact the "Special Sales Department" at the address above.

Decoding Revelation / Zavicar III. -- 1st ed.
ISBN 978-1-63357-282-9

Scripture quotations marked NIV are taken from the Holy Bible, New International Version®, NIV®. Copyright © 1973, 1978, 1984, 2011 by Biblica, Inc.™ Used by permission of Zondervan. All rights reserved worldwide. www.zondervan.com The "NIV" and "New International Version" are trademarks registered in the United States Patent and Trademark Office by Biblica, Inc.™

"Excerpts from the English translation of the Catechism of the Catholic Church for use in the United States of America Copyright © 1994, United States Catholic Conference, Inc. -- Libreria Editrice Vaticana. Used with Permission. English translation of the Catechism of the Catholic Church: Modifications from the Editio Typica copyright © 1997, United States Conference of Catholic Bishops—Libreria Editrice Vaticana."

Contents

Background and Introduction 1

Really Lord, The Books of Revelation and Daniel? 11

More Directions 23

Vision Proof 35

Theological Stew 45

Two Witnesses 57

Jesus and the Scribe 71

Guidance for the Church 87

What Must Take Place 97

Success of the Church 105

The Church Future 113

The Transition and Seventh Seal 123

Four Trumpets of the Reign of Jesus 133

The Time of the End and Three Woes 145

Two Witnesses Welcome the Gentiles 155

The Woman and the "Seven" of Jesus 175

The Reign of the RCC 193

The End of the Reign of the RCC 209

The Bowls of Wrath 221

The Great Prostitute, the Beast, and Death 241

The Transition to Jesus—Heaven Is Silent 255

Judgment and Rewards 263

The Warning 273

Background and Introduction

For just about three years now I have been receiving dreams or visions that direct and guide me to conduct and report on very thorough and unique Bible studies. Some of these visions have obvious meanings which I immediately understand because they direct me to information or conclusions about sections of Scripture that I am in the process of trying to understand or unravel. But this is not always the case—some visions end up being a piece of a bigger puzzle that takes me time to solve. If I don't understand the meaning of a vision, I write down the details to allow me to periodically return to it to see if the Holy Spirit has opened my mind yet. If not, it stays on the list until I understand the message. Ultimately, over time the messages of *all* my visions become clear, and at some point, I end up saying to myself, "Oh yeah—now I get it! Thank you, Lord, for helping me to understand what the Holy Spirit has been trying to tell me." I hope you noticed that I gave credit to Jesus and the Holy Spirit for my visions. I will address this aspect of these investigations and books as we end this chapter with some administrative issues.

I had the following vision as I was completing the analysis and summary of the book of Daniel:

DECODING REVELATION

February 7, 2023—I was being driven down a winding road by a chauffeur and as I sat in the back seat of a limo, I stared out the window to witness numerous individuals walking next to the road. They were not all the same people, but they were dressed alike and had the same type of haircut—appearing like ancient keepers of the books, monks, or even librarians. They seemed to be struggling in their journey as they were sweating in the hot sun, and they all had the same look of distress on their faces. As I stared out the window at them and we passed them by, they stared back with a look that I couldn't quite figure out—almost as though they were angry at me. Then I got out of bed, wrote this vision down, and prayed to God for the meaning.

As I mentioned previously, sometimes the message is easy to understand and other times I must wait for more direction and piece the puzzle together. This was a vision that the Lord had me, with a bit of reflection, immediately understand. It was the Lord who was taking me on a journey—he was the chauffeur, and I was the passenger who was in the back seat of the limousine being taken for a ride. The journey I was on was the scripture investigations and book writing that I was performing. As we went along the winding road, I was protected in the car indicating that the Lord was letting me rest in peace on my journey and was with me as I kept doing my work. Although I was at peace in my journey, I could see that everyone else on the road that we passed by was not. Those we passed by were

Background and Introduction

in anguish and I sensed trouble, but I wasn't sure whether their grief was directed at me or if it was a symptom of their difficult journey. We were both headed in the same direction, but my journey was blessed by Jesus and was much easier than what they were experiencing.

I reasoned that they were in turmoil because my results were causing them grief. They are keepers of the word—the theologians and the studious ones, but I was not. They didn't like it that I was getting a ride from Jesus because they had worked hard to understand the words of scripture, and here I was—not one of them with their education, background, and experience—claiming to be interpreting scripture by being guided by Jesus and the Holy Spirit. Who was I to analyze scripture and tell them and the world what scripture meant? I was a nobody and it didn't matter to them that Jesus was at the wheel taking me for a ride. Not only that, these studious-looking people on the side of the road didn't like my results. I've written three previous books and they all focus on exposing the negative effects that tradition has had on the church, and these men outside the vehicle are on the side of tradition that has infiltrated scripture as though it is the Word of God.

As we reported in previous books, although Jesus condemned tradition and the disciples warned against it, the church has embraced it and in many cases the people of God are trying to maneuver through it to find Jesus. This is not an isolated problem because *all* churches are teaching tradition that has been embedded into the Word of God. You heard that right—*all* churches embrace the condemned made–up stories of tradition in their worship of Jesus. For example, every time a preacher reads scripture from a book called the Gospel of

Matthew, then describes to the church how the author of the Gospel of Matthew was a tax collector named Matthew who left his table to blindly follow Jesus then wrote the first Gospel that captured his experiences with Jesus—they are teaching tradition—unproven stories created by people. What you have been told is a story made up by early church fathers who others passed along through the years as though it is the truth. These people created a story about Matthew, edited a few choice words in scripture, then named a Gospel after this made-up tax collector and placed it first in the organization of the New Testament books. Why? Because it benefited them!

Since the completion of my first investigation, I grimace whenever I hear the story of Matthew the tax collector because I know that tradition is being taught, and whoever is preaching the sermon is straying from sticking to the Word of God. The story of a tax collector leaving everything to follow Jesus is true, however, that is where the truth ends. There is no evidence that the author of the Gospel called Matthew was a tax collector. We have a similar scenario for the Gospels of Mark and Luke—there is no proof that the claimed authors wrote them. These are stories of tradition that were created at the start of the church to allow a group of evil men to take complete control of the church of Jesus Christ. The Holy Spirit started me on this journey three years ago to expose these facts. Now you understand why I'm in the vehicle being chauffeured by Jesus and the keepers of the Word are upset and in turmoil. They are not saying anything to counter what I've written, but they are in grief because my results are upsetting the theologians and teachers of the Word. If you are interested in the background and proof of this claim, please see the results of the

Background and Introduction

first two investigations for documented proof and evidence for who the real Gospel authors were (*Course Corrections to Faith and Identify the Real Gospel Authors* and *The Early Church Father Catholic Fraud*).

God knew tradition would be the path that evil false teachers would take to gain control of the church of Jesus Christ—this was explicitly embedded in the visions that both Daniel and John received. For example, John wrote a warning from Jesus about those who will use tradition to change the meaning of prophecy in Revelation 22:18. We'll get into the details of this toward the end of this book, but first, let me address another important aspect of that vision I received on February 7, 2022; I just happened to receive it exactly one year to the day after I received a vision the Lord presented me to get me started on my investigation to analyze and interpret prophecy. In the next chapter, I'll address the details of that vision I refer to as the "then it happened" because it was an eye-opener—a vision that opened my mind to unravel and understand prophecy. Before we get into those details in the next chapter, let me first take you on a short detour and close out this introductory chapter with some administrative issues I need to present to help you through the remainder of this book.

First, I need to address that this investigation has been split into two parts because the message is so complex and difficult to present. I found out as the investigation into prophecy continued that the two subject Bible books of study, Daniel and Revelation, can *only* be understood when they are analyzed together, but the books are so complex and different that the results could not be presented in one book. This investigation required an analysis of both Daniel and Revelation together and

this investigation has resulted in two books that capture the results. We completed our analysis of the book of Daniel and presented it in a book called *Unraveling Daniel*. That first book focused on the prophecy in the book of Daniel, but it also included analyses of some specific prophecy from the book of Revelation that was necessary to fully explain Daniel. Although this book focuses on Revelation, out of necessity we will periodically refer to *Unraveling Daniel* to support the understanding of Revelation prophecy.

Second, as you may have already noticed if you read my previous books, I frequently refer to more than one person working on these investigations—I periodically use the terms *"we"* and *"us"* sprinkled throughout my books rather than *"I"* and *"me."* This is intentional because I am not working on this investigation alone—if I were, I wouldn't have the results and conclusions we are presenting. The Holy Spirit is guiding and directing me in this work and the use of these pronouns is a depiction of the joint team effort to provide an accurate and thorough interpretation of scripture.

Third, to be consistent, whenever I present Daniel and Revelation scripture and analysis, I will use the New International Version (NIV) Study Bible's interpretation and translation copyright 1985, 2011 by Zondervan. The copyright information has been presented on a copyright page. Having consistent translations is an important aspect of my investigations. By using the same translation for our in–depth analysis of prophecy, we can ensure that we are using consistent translations so as not to skew our work to reach a preconceived or desired outcome. Our full intent is to analyze scripture to find the true meaning of what was written nearly 2,000 years

Background and Introduction

ago. On the flip side, to keep from having more copyright paperwork to complete, unless specifically noted, all additional scripture from the other books of the Bible will be taken from the copyright free World English Bible (WEB). Every now and then there are interesting and subtle differences between interpretations so when I need to consider this and refer to another translation, I will inform you and document the exception.

Fourth, as we go through our analysis you will see two different patterns used to present the meaning of scripture. For example, since the focus of this book is on unraveling the mystery of the book of Revelation, let's use the first verse of that book to demonstrate what we mean:

> The revelation from Jesus Christ, which God gave him to show his servants what must soon take place. He made it known by sending his angel to his servant John, (Revelation 1:1)

Later in this book, you will be provided an analysis similar to the following:

> Initially John is told about "what must soon take place." This must be a reference to what will be covered in this Revelation on "heaven time." We discussed heaven time in our review of the book of Daniel, but we will return to it when we analyze Revelation 8:1. As a prelude, an hour of heaven time is equal to 2,300 years of earth time, therefore verse 1:1, "what must soon take place," is referring to *all* the New Covenant. This prophecy will address the entire hour of Je-

sus from his birth to the coming of the eternal church at the time of the end (what must soon take place).

I presented scripture in the analysis in two different ways. In the first sentence, the words taken from scripture were presented in quotation marks as we presented the scripture words *in the sentence* to help explain the meaning. At the end of the description, we continued our explanation of verse 1:1 by explaining the meaning of the scripture and included in parentheses the words from scripture that we are explaining. We will use both these techniques to walk you through scripture as we interpret Revelation prophecy.

Fifth and finally, a vision that I will describe later told me that *every* word of scripture is important, therefore, we will analyze *each* verse of the prophecy in Revelation with only minor exceptions. We will *not omit* scripture because it is initially difficult to understand. We will go through the book of Revelation verse-by-verse looking at every word to put it into context with surrounding scripture and scripture from other books of the Bible to ensure we are providing the full and intended meaning of prophecy. Only when we come upon scripture that repeats an earlier message such as a visual of God or the details of a prayer, will we not present the verses in this book. Without exception, when we do not present verses, we will explain why. This will result in every verse being discussed and interpreted, but not all will be presented.

In summary, I have done my best to follow the Holy Spirit's direction, therefore, I fully believe that the interpretation of Revelation presented in this book is correct. However, there

Background and Introduction

are isolated sections that are very difficult to understand, and the Holy Spirit may be telling you something different. If you believe there to be another meaning, I am interested in your thoughts, so please feel free to contact me. Now to the visions that brought me to Revelation—the "then it happened!"

Really Lord, The Books of Revelation and Daniel?

*I*MENTIONED IN THE INTRODUCTION to this book that there was a powerful "then it happened!" moment that is the whole basis for this investigation into prophecy. I had just completed an investigation of a fraud committed in the early church and found that this fraud is still greatly affecting the church, then I received another vision that indicated the Holy Spirit was not through with me yet. The Lord had a message in prophecy for me. Once you see how the books of Revelation and Daniel provide clear and precise warnings about the fraud we had just identified and exposed in *The Early Church Father Catholic Fraud* you will see why the Lord prompted this investigation next. I carefully chose the word *"prompted"* because I rebelled—I didn't want to investigate prophecy.

The "then it happened!" is a bit of a story, so I will need to present the story from the beginning. As I already stated, I have been receiving visions that have been directing me in Bible studies for about three years. When I completed the second investigation, I had leftover data from the first two books. I was looking forward to a bit of brain rest so I started to assemble the data into a third book that *would not* require another investigation—I was hoping for a "down period" in which I could easily tie up loose ends with a third book. I had all the data, therefore, all the groundwork was completed for a third book that would address tradition and corruption in the existing church. However, because I wanted to be certain that what I intended to review was what God wanted me to look at, I prayed for more direction from the Holy Spirit. My prayers were answered very quickly with the following vision from the Holy Spirit:

> January 16, 2022—I met a man who is wealthy but meek who welcomed me into his home. I am going through his financial documents, but I feel like he asked me over to go through martial arts technique together. He knows judo and jujitsu.

I'm sure you are saying, "But wait, John, what kind of message is that? How can this vision be an answer to your prayers?" I wondered, too, because this vision didn't seem to fit into the final pieces of the puzzle that I was working on to wrap up *The Early Church Father Catholic Fraud,* nor did it appear to be related to the other data I was assembling for a third easy book. I documented this vision because I knew I would understand it in due time, then I continued to wrap up that second book and assemble the documentation for the next message—the easy investigation and follow-up book.

Then I received another vision that I wrote down:

> January 25, 2022—I need to turn to the book of Revelation.

Really Lord, The Books of Revelation and Daniel?

Now I'll bet you're really confused. If I'm only writing down the details of visions I don't understand as I stated in the last chapter, then why did I write this one down? It's obvious the message is very clear—the Lord was telling me to investigate the book of Revelation! My next job was to start looking at the book of Revelation, right? Yes, the message was clear but there was one problem with it; I didn't like it! I didn't want to look at that puzzle called the book of Revelation! Here comes the music from the movie *Jaws* with the driving bass . . . bum . . . bum . . . bum . . . bum . . . indicating that something ominous is about to happen. I was getting a clear message from the Holy Spirit for the direction I was to take but I thought the Holy Spirit was screwing up. You see, I had already read through the book of Revelation several times and it never made any sense to me. I even purchased a study book written by a great pastor and theologian named Skip Heitzig with the title *You Can Understand the Book of Revelation*. Sorry, Skip, you're a great pastor and I love your teaching, but after reading your book, I didn't understand the book of Revelation any better.

The book of Revelation made no sense to me, and I wasn't excited about the new direction I was being shown. Was I hoping to get fired? Maybe, because I sure didn't want to look at the book of Revelation and I was getting tired of writing books on faith anyway. Many experts much smarter than me with great theological backgrounds had already written their commentary on the book of Revelation and they included their own hypothetical summaries and conclusions. What could I possibly add to existing commentary? Besides, who cares if the interpretations contained in other books weren't clear, nobody can explain the meaning of prophecy in that book anyway . . . or can they?

In the meantime, I kept updating my wife Karen about my visions and when I told her the latest—that I was being directed to start an investigation into prophecy contained in the book of Revelation—she didn't seem too thrilled. She really didn't like the results I had obtained from the Gospel-author investigation and certainly didn't appreciate that I had reported on corruption in the church in the second book. She was a Christian since her youth, and I was shaking things up by claiming that the Gospel authors were intentionally misnamed so that a group of evil people could take over the church. This meant that the preachers and experts in the word had been and still were being fooled by the injection of tradition into the church and this wasn't a palatable consideration.

When I mentioned to her that I was asked to investigate the book of Revelation, she snapped back at me, "If you're going to look at the book of Revelation, then you also need to look at the book of Daniel." I walked away frustrated because Karen was adding fuel to the fire—I didn't want to investigate the book of Revelation and I certainly didn't want to dig into an Old Testament book that I knew had more confusing incomprehensible prophecy in it. Then I received another vision:

> February 1, 2022—I woke up this morning with the Holy Spirit telling me I needed to do a comparison between Daniel and John, just like I did with the Gospel writers.

Really Lord, The Books of Revelation and Daniel?

I said I was frustrated with Karen when she mentioned the book of Daniel but, in reality, I wasn't just frustrated—I was downright mad. I already didn't want to look at Revelation and the book of Daniel was no better. The only thing the book of Daniel had going for it was that it was a lot shorter—twelve chapters verses the twenty-two chapters in the book of Revelation. Now the Lord was telling me that Karen was right, and I had to expand the investigation to include the book of Daniel. What do you think I did next? I did nothing—I made no changes—I kept on assembling the data for the third book that I *wanted to be* my next assignment.

Then, a few strange things happened. I still struggled for direction with my now expanded assignment, but the guilt was overcoming me, so I relented and started reading the book of Revelation to somewhat satisfy my commitment to the Lord and, as expected, I quickly became overwhelmed and frustrated. Then the Holy Spirit recognized my struggles and provided much needed direction. About a week later, I received and documented the "then it happened!" vision:

> February 7, 2022—We were away in Daytona with Barbara [my sister] and got home yesterday afternoon. I woke up this morning with the Spirit telling me that the book of Revelation is not about the end of the world, it is only about the Church. Focus on this and the answers to what I am to do next will come.

Wow—what a message! Remember I claimed that I received the keys to unravel prophecy a year to the date before I received that vision on February 7, 2023? This is it! Everything I needed to proceed and unravel the centuries-old mysteries of Revelation and Daniel was just handed to me in a vision. Then, a few days later, on February 9th, I received another wake-up call from the Holy Spirit. I got up and immediately wrote down the following message:

> February 9, 2022—I went to bed last night praying that what I am supposed to know will become evident as I am told what to do next. I woke up with the thought to write down all the references to the church and it will become evident that the book of Revelation is all about the church.

The Holy Spirit has now told me twice that the book of Revelation is *all* about the church—not partially about the church—it's *all about the church*. I'll repeat this guidance for even more emphasis:

February 7, 2022: ". . . the book of Revelation is not about the end of the world, it is only about the Church."

February 9, 2022: " . . . the book of Revelation is *all* about the church."

Initially, I had no idea how valuable this one small bit of direction obtained from these last two visions was to understand the message of prophecy. How's that for some direction and help? In addition, I still had the vision of January 16th about the wealthy but meek man to contend with and solve.

After writing down these messages, I knew I had to go to the end of the Bible to look in the index for the word *"church,"* so I

Really Lord, The Books of Revelation and Daniel?

opened my NIV Study Bible up and was taken directly to a page where the word *"church"* was in an index. This time though, the index seemed different. I had been using this Study Bible for several years, but didn't recognize this index labeled *"Index of Topics."* I had never used this index before and didn't even know it existed. This was very unusual but interesting. It had a detailed summary of the church, so I typed in the following summary from that index description contained in the NIV:

- God's building
- God's field
- the temple of the Holy Spirit
- a pure virgin
- the Jerusalem that is above
- the Israel of God
- the body of Christ
- a chosen people
- a royal priesthood
- a holy nation
- God's special possession
- the flock of God, and,
- the wife of the Lamb.

All the references to scripture in that index are from the New Testament and this made sense to me because one of the identification labels for the church is the *"body of Christ"* and, although the Old Testament pointed to Jesus, the New Testament is all about Jesus. Jesus is the new covenant with God, therefore, although the church has many descriptions, the church is all about Jesus, or rather, the church *is* Jesus because it is impossible to separate Jesus from his church and followers!

I was well on my way with an investigation into the book of Revelation and felt like I now had some direction. However, there was still one major problem—I was already overwhelmed with starting to look at the book of Revelation and I still didn't want to add the book of Daniel to my investigation. I hadn't even looked at that book yet, then finally on March 6, 2022, the Holy Spirit had enough of my stubbornness and put circumstances in my life to get me on the right track. I woke up at my current usual time of 4:15 a.m., then laid in bed trying to get more sleep. As usual, this didn't go well so I got out of bed, grabbed my prayer notes, fired up the coffee pot, and prayed. As if in a blind routine, after praying I went to grab my computer in the dark to start typing. I immediately found things to be different that morning. Instead of my computer being charged up and ready to go, it wasn't even on the charger—apparently, I had forgotten to hook it up before I went to bed. This shouldn't have been a problem though because I had barely used the computer the day before, so when I pushed the start button and nothing happened, I was worried that my hard drive had failed. I quickly patted myself on the back for sending myself an email the day before with an updated version of this book that I had written early the previous morning, just in case my hard drive had fried.

Having a dead computer in the morning was a first so I shook my head a bit frustrated and plugged in the computer. I pushed the start button and presto—the computer turned on. I wasn't sure how the battery had drained because as I stated I hadn't used the computer much the day before, but I accepted

Really Lord, The Books of Revelation and Daniel?

the situation, then turned the computer off to let it charge. Why didn't I just start writing again using the computer as it charged? Because Karen has a habit of "hiding stuff." She had coincidentally wrapped the charging cord around a table leg several times to hide the cord behind a plant, so I decided it would be a nightmare to move the charger to my desk and have it charge as I continued documenting results. I decided to read scripture this morning rather than type. I had been reading the book of Revelation for several days now and was a bit exhausted and needed a change so reluctantly I accepted that maybe it was time to open the Bible up to the book of Daniel and start reading.

Like always, God won! My computer didn't work, so finally I gave in, started to study the book of Daniel, and boy was I glad that I did. God had to drain my computer battery and have Karen intricately hide the cord to provide the final push, but it worked, and afterward I was thankful. As I read the book of Daniel with the guidance that this prophecy also *must be all about the church,* my interest in the connection to the book of Revelation increased. I continued reading then finally reached chapter 7 that described a vision of the future that Daniel had. My interest peaked immediately because Daniel described his visions in a way that made sense to me. For a long time, I was at a loss for words to describe my visions, but Daniel described the gift of receiving visions perfectly:

> In the first year of Belshazzar king of Babylon, Daniel had a dream, and visions passed through his mind as he was lying in bed. He wrote down the substance of his dream. (Daniel 7:1)

DECODING REVELATION

There is a fine line between dreams and visions. Daniel calls it a *"dream"* but then states that in response to the dream he had visions that "passed through his mind as he was lying in bed." His dream led him to visions that he would have to ponder the meaning of to decipher the meaning of his dream.

There could not be a better explanation of how these dreams and visions came to me. First, let me state that all my life I have not had dreams. But now, after turning to the Lord I was frequently waking up with very short dreams in my head—sometimes even just snapshots, then continued to lie in bed while receiving visions about the meaning of the dream. I wasn't dreaming but I wasn't completely awake either. As I received my messages, I just laid in bed thinking about what was going through my head and wondering about it. Eventually, I would get out of bed and start using the message if I understood it or writing it down for future reference if I didn't. Even if this was the only result from the book of Daniel that I obtained, it was worth the journey to it. However, this was just the opening of the door. I quickly found out that these two books of prophecy, Daniel and Revelation, could not be analyzed without considering the other—they are highly dependent on each other. I started thinking that *Decoding Revelation* would be the first book, but the Lord eventually showed me that my assumption was wrong and *Unraveling Daniel* was to be first. Now, here I am wrapping up the investigation with the second book, *Decoding Revelation*.

There's only one loose end before we leave this chapter—I still haven't explained the vision that I received on January 16, 2022. This vision will provide you the proof that we have a God in heaven who understands us better than we know ourselves!

Really Lord, The Books of Revelation and Daniel?

At first, as I stated, that vision didn't seem make sense, but in summary, the vision told me that God knew what I was going to do before I did it. He knew I'd be frustrated and rebellious about accepting my next assignment to look at prophecy, so before he gave me the assignment, he told me what my reaction to the assignment would be. The vision of January 16 was God's way of showing me just how much he knew me and knew the future. It's not a coincidence that prophecy in Daniel and Revelation is all about God telling us what will happen in the future. It's been a little while since you read it, so let me repeat the vision for ease of review:

> January 16, 2022—I met a man who is wealthy but meek who welcomed me into his home. I am going through his financial documents, but I feel like he asked me over to go through martial arts technique together. He knows judo and jujitsu.

I am interested in both financial investments and martial arts, and I spend time trying to learn and understand both. However, I know a lot more about martial arts than I do about financial investments. I have benefited from the extensive training under well-respected and knowledgeable martial arts teachers Grandmaster Eugene Humesky from Ann Arbor, Michigan, and Grandmaster Abel Villareal from Austin, Texas. In addition, I have been teaching martial arts for nearly fifty years. I am nowhere near that competent in my understanding of finances. I have been known to dabble in financial investments and retirement planning, and even put together a pretty good spreadsheet that helped me and some others retire early, but in no way am I considered an expert.

In the vision I received on January 25th, I was given my next assignment, but I ignored it to focus on the next subject *I wanted to focus on*—the easy one to give my brain a rest. The earlier vision from January 16th told me that God knew I was initially going to reject the command of God to start reviewing the book of Revelation, and I was going to continue doing my own thing. On January 25th, the Lord invited me into his house to show me something (prophecy/martial arts) but I walked into his house and did what I wanted to do (financials). I requested help from God for direction through prayer, then when they were answered with a vision, I ignored the directions. The ultimate grand master of knowledge, Jesus, had something he wanted to share with me, but I arrogantly rejected this information, walked into his house, and started looking at what I wanted to look at—financial information. Note that I was told I would reject my assignment on January 16th—a week and a half before I was given the assignment on January 25th. How's that for an example of God thoroughly knowing my thoughts, actions, and even the future? This alone should have you believing God and following his son Jesus.

I continued to read both books and, as I compared the prophecy of Daniel to that contained in the book of Revelation, I was quickly amazed at what the Lord had chosen me to understand and document. The only downside was that the message was so long and complex it had to be split into two separate books, and this is part two of that message, called *Decoding Revelation*.

3

More Directions

*I*N THE OPENING CHAPTERS, I captured visions that were leading me to investigate the books of Daniel and Revelation to unravel prophecy. My direction and guidance from the Holy Spirit did not stop with those visions in February and March of 2022—in fact, my guidance for this investigation was just starting. Prior to receiving additional visions, I was moved by the Holy Spirit to do some reflecting. A few weeks after the Holy Spirit gave me my next assignment, we received a visit from our good friends who lived in Michigan. Our friends wanted to escape the cold weather in Michigan and what better place to do that than to visit central/south Florida in February. There's nothing hidden in that message—it's cold there and warm here, so it's obvious that people will travel to see us in the winter.

As always, having visitors didn't change my routine—every day the Holy Spirit woke me up early and eager to write; the *"eager"* word was a joke if you didn't pick up on that—*early* and *eager* are two words that shouldn't be used in the same sentence. I don't think I'm the only person on the planet who is working for the Lord who wouldn't mind a bit more sleep to feel better focused! After a few nights of our friend's visit, we stayed up a little later than usual and I wondered if this was going to affect my limited hours of sleep that I struggled to obtain every night. I had my usual bathroom break at about 3:30 a.m. which

normally meant it was time to get up and get started writing for the Lord. I fought to go back to sleep like I always did because I was still tired and wanted more rest. Today was different. I fell back asleep then was surprised to wake up and see that the sun had already risen. My friends and wife, Karen, would wake up soon and we would have our normal debate on what to eat for breakfast, then turn to discuss the plan of the day, or "*POD*," as it had been referred to during my working past.

I felt that the Lord was calling me to go to the beach that morning but there was a strong wind blowing from the north due to a cold front that had passed through during the night. We all stepped outside and, when we did, they realized the park would be a better choice for them because the park was a few blocks from the beach, and they wouldn't get the blasts of the cold ocean breeze. I was still being called to the beach but wasn't sure why. I knew it would be an uncomfortable walk on the beach with temps in the mid-fifties and a strong steady north wind blowing at twenty miles per hour with greater gusts. I decided I had to follow where I was being led, therefore, we split up; they took the golf cart to the park, and I dusted off my old bicycle that hadn't been used in several months that was now retired to the shed, then set out for the short one-third-mile ride to the beach.

As I headed out the door in shorts and a sleeveless T-shirt, I wrapped a long-sleeved thermal t-shirt around my waist just in case I felt cold. I was only a few hundred feet down the road when I was hit by a blast of cold air and decided to put the thermal shirt on, so while pedaling I pulled the T-shirt over my head, blinding me for just a few short moments. I thought to myself, hmm . . . I can still ride a bike no handed without stopping to put a shirt on or remove it—cool! I flashed back to a memory of about ten years ago when while riding my bike no-handed down our street some youngsters about three or four years old pointed me out to their parents as they yelled their praises at me for being able to ride without hands. I saw myself as a bad example and quickly grabbed the handlebars yelling back at them, "Don't try this at home." Determined to follow my instincts, I arrived at the beach, parked the bike, then strategically started walking north to head into the wind first to get the coldest portion of the walk out of the way first.

    I quickly realized that walking directly into the wind was going to be a big challenge, but as I looked around, I was immediately stricken with the reason I was being called to the beach. Even though it seemed brutally cold, the beauty of the waves, the birds fishing for their breakfast, and the large offshore swells reminded me that my walks on the beach were for my quiet time with the Lord. I started praying and quickly forgot about how the wind was blasting me with a chill. I noticed that some small, blue, balloon-like man-of-wars had washed up on the shore creating hazards, so I carefully avoided the intermittent hazards and continued walking barefoot down the beach. I noticed a seagull dive into the water and grab a snack then devour it in midflight without dropping it back to the sea, then fly off in peace. Things were different here on the Atlantic Coast. In Corpus Christi, Texas, our former residence, the seagulls would loudly squawk and fight over every morsel they could find but here there were fewer seagulls, and they seemed to live in harmony.

    My time with the Lord made me forget how my legs and face were getting numb from the cold wind. As I walked down the beach, I thought about all the work I was facing with this new investigation, so I started praying for more of the sometimes-foggy directions from the Holy Spirit. I was quickly reminded by the Lord how I had received the vision of the church index in my NIV Study Bible, then I was told that I needed to revisit the index descriptions of the church and tie it to the book of Revelation. Next, I remembered how I was told that the book of Revelation is all about the church. I quickly had a path forward; the first step in the process was to reread the book of Revelation with the church in mind. Like the Gospel authors Matthew, Mark, and Luke, I felt that the interpretations of prophecy were not being told accurately, because why else would the Spirit be prompting me to investigate and closely analyze it?

Scripture describes the church as many things, so I realized that I needed to keep an open mind as I went through my review. I reached my half-way walk marker at a blue A-frame house that we had used our GPS to determine the distance of the walk at one mile. As soon as I turned around to head back, the sun removed my sensation of being cold and brought me immediate peace. I thought about that and related it to the warmth of God and how Jesus told us that he is the light of the world. Change the word *"sun"* to *"Son"* and I had an explanation for my peace—the "Son" was shining on me!

As I continued walking back, I started noticing the wind blowing the sand at the back of my legs feeling like I was getting sandblasted. I also noticed that this negative aspect of the wind and blowing sand was also providing me safety from the scattered, dying man-of-war that were now coated with the sand but stuck out like clumps of sand—I could no longer see the little blue balloons, but they were still visible as clumps of sand

More Directions

gathered around them. I rationalized that although the wind was causing me a bit of pain from the sand blasting my legs there was solace in it too as it was keeping me safe from the stinging of the dying man-of-war. It made me remember that even though I had peace in the Lord, there were still going to be painful experiences on this earth during my journey the Holy Spirit had me on. Yes, my work will cause grief and pain and it is going to be difficult, but if I continue to walk with the Lord, I will find peace through the pain. Jesus gave people his church to help with the pain and keep us in peace through a sharing of faith in Jesus and I was comforted by this.

As I was close to finishing my walk with the Lord, the message of what I was to do became clear. People tend to try to understand every little detail in prophecy in a literal sense, but this is an error. Look at my visions and how simple they seemed to be as compared to the books of visions that John and Daniel wrote about. Still, although my visions were simple, I had to put them in context to what I was currently addressing to understand the meaning of what I was being shown. As an example, I was not really invited into the Lord's house for a martial arts lesson. In addition, I wasn't really driving down a winding road in a limousine with Jesus at the wheel. Just like my visions had messages in them for me, John's visions will be revealed by understanding the message the Lord was giving him about the future of the church—and not taking them too literally. The characteristics of a creature will mean something to explain what the creature is and the message from it. A mountain won't get thrown into the sea, but it will have a meaning to it that can be put into context with the surrounding prophecy. That's a key point—to accurately understand John's vision, all aspects of his vision will need to be put into context with the surrounding scripture and the overall message of prophecy that is a uniform and coherent message all about the church.

John's movie must be taken as a whole—the pieces must fit together. It made sense then that if the book of Revelation was all about the church, then John's movie provides readers with the history and future of the church. Each piece of John's movie will support the rest of the visions; it will be one vision that is about the church, but there will be separate visions that clarify parts of the message. At the risk of repeating myself, John's visions are not to be taken too literally—they are to be considered figuratively. One-hundred-pound hailstorms falling from the sky does not necessarily mean that there will be big balls of hail striking the earth, but then again, it might! This last concept is not an easy one for those who have been taught the same message over and over through the years. John, seeing a blazing star falling from the sky or a mountain thrown into the sea has everyone looking up waiting for comets and meteors to damage the earth, but this is not the intent of the visions. The stars are the light of Jesus shining through the darkness of night, therefore, stars falling and the moon losing its light are representative of the light of Jesus being removed from the world. In addition, John had no idea what certain visions likely represented. Imagine John describing weapons of war such as bombs, bomber planes, and Humvees with blazing bullets streaming across that horizon. Try to explain a high-rise condo building to someone who lived in the forest their whole life and was isolated from civilization. A high-rise condo might look like a mountain to that person, or it might look like something else.

More Directions

The Lord showed me that there were at least thirteen ways to describe the church of Jesus Christ in the New Testament. The Lord also told me that the book of Revelation is all about the church. Now the Lord had shown me how we should not take too literally the descriptions in the book of Revelation—I needed to keep an open mind and think outside of the box while understanding that the book of Revelation is all about the church of Jesus Christ. The message may be confusing because there are so many ways to describe Jesus' church, but with patience and focusing on these simple guidelines, the message will become clear.

I mentioned that I also had more visions to help direct me. In keeping with my theme to demonstrate the input of the Holy Spirit, I will present a few more of these visions that helped me in my quest to unravel the mysteries of prophecy in the books of Daniel and Revelation. As the investigation was kicking into high gear, I received the following visions needing interpretation later:

> April 3, 2022—I was in someone's home that didn't belong to me. I was messing with the stereo, trying to get to the right station to find my location. I turned the knob and lost the location we were in. I flipped through a bit trying to find our location and just as I found it, I noticed a car in front—the owner was home. I noticed the owner standing outside with her back to the house while Karen talked to her. The front door was open, and the stereo console had been moved from its original place. I was trying

to figure out how to get the stereo back in its place and get out without her knowing I was in her home. Has the book of Revelation been edited by false teachers too? I think the Lord was telling me that the directions in prophecy are not specifically related to where—it can mean the magnitude or spread of whatever is being discussed.

Even though I was only a few months into the investigation when I received this vision, I knew the Lord was telling me that the presence of false teachers in the church would be overwhelming in the future. The false teachers were predicted to be in the Lord's house rearranging prophecy to support their personal gain. Just like we had found for the renaming of the Gospel authors, we were going to find corruption in prophecy that was the result of false teachers who were intent on taking over the church.

In my vision, Karen and I were uninvited intruders just like the corrupt church leaders were not permitted to enter the church, but they entered the church and took it over anyway. No matter how much they tried to remove the evidence of their intrusion from detection, it didn't matter because just like my vision, they couldn't completely cover their tracks. Those corrupting the church don't want anyone to know their deceptions, so they tried to completely cover them up—but they were unsuccessful. Let me clarify this—they have been successful for many years by creating stories of tradition that point preachers away from understanding who the beast is and why it exists. Stories of a future tribulation and Antichrist are intended

More Directions

to have people look away from closely examining prophecy to determine that the beast already lives amongst the church. The meaning of prophecy has been corrupted for many years to point away from the false teachers and we will explain how this has happened as we continue through our verse-by-verse analysis. The beasts are easily explained by looking at history, yet most in the church are silent about the connection, and why is this? Because stories of tradition hide the truth and a very powerful church considered by many to be the one true church of Jesus Christ controlled the Word and the message for many years. Their effects are ongoing even today.

Finally, in that vision I was concerned about what my location was, but it didn't matter because it had nothing to do with the fact that I had entered someone else's home without their permission. I was trying to tune a radio to find my location in my dream, but a radio station could only indirectly provide me with my location. We will find the details of corruption wrapped up and described with generalized locations (east, west, north, and south) that in some cases will be presented to describe the magnitude of the effects. Directional prophecy will, like the rest, need to be considered in context with the rest of the message. The directional meaning might be intended to present the magnitude of something—something from all four locations will mean that something is from the whole world. Or, like from the book of Daniel review, we will find that Jesus came from the east and this makes sense because the sun (Son) rises in the east! With Jesus coming from the east, something out of the west—the opposite direction—will be opposed to Jesus.

Then I received another vision:

DECODING REVELATION

> April 15, 2022—The Lion and his message are calm and peaceful.

Remember that the true lion of the tribe of Judah, Jesus, is a message of tranquility. When there is peace and tranquility presented in prophecy it will be all about Jesus. Less than a week later, I received another vision that provided a summary of the investigation:

> April 21, 2022—I was in a hotel room or some place that was very dirty. I was spraying a cleaner all over the bathroom shower or tub and the dirt was foaming off, then I was going to spray the tub with water and wash away the dirt. I was shown and told that the book of Revelation is simple, and the message is very clear. Don't complicate the interpretation. It is all about the dirty church and it needs cleansing. It is time to wash away the dirt.

Do you think the message of the book of Revelation was being spelled out clearly for me by the Holy Spirit? The book of Revelation, in summary, will provide the entire history and future of the Church but it is going to be a dirty story that will shock you if you haven't tuned in to the numerous references to false teachers and corruption of the church in scripture. I had a relatively simple message to deliver about the church: The Lord is telling us through prophecy that the church is stained with corruption, and it is time to wash away the dirt to expose the truth in scripture.

More Directions

The message of prophecy is very clear—Jesus will come to bring peace to the world, but the world will reject his words, attack him and his followers, and cause great turmoil in the world. The church will be corrupted from the beginning by the presence of evil in it from the start. As you will see later presented in Revelation, at first when Jesus commissioned his church and the apostles started it, the church was pure like a virgin. God protected the church at the beginning to allow it to get its footing so as not to be eliminated by false teachers, but then the flood gates were opened, and the false teachers attacked. The books of Daniel and Revelation describe the changes to the church over time as the false teachers infiltrate then persecute those in the church of Jesus Christ. The church is taken over completely by the great false church we now know as the Roman Catholic Church (RCC) who will persecute and execute the followers of Jesus. After a long period of time of persecution—1,300 years to be exact—the church created by the apostles, the Apostolic Church (APC), will be revived when Jesus returns to earth to reign over his church. Then, after a thousand-year reign of Jesus, he will destroy the church and the earth and replace it with his eternal church. These are all details of the future written in the book of Daniel that we presented in *Unraveling Daniel*. The predictions, except for the arrival of the eternal church, have already been proven to have come true. In *Decoding Revelation*, we *confirm* and expanded upon what we have discovered and documented from Daniel.

I had my marching orders for the next puzzle I had been asked to solve. The Lord had provided steppingstones to take me from message to successive message. The first steppingstone was an investigation that exposed that two of the Gospels had been misnamed. The second steppingstone was an investigation that exposed a third Gospel to have been misnamed and the misnamed Gospels became the basis for a fraud committed by the founders of the RCC to completely take over the APC. The third steppingstone reveals that prophecy predicted the devastating effects of false teachers on the church. Prophecy also proves that God has set times and knew exactly what his creation would do to Jesus and his church. Come along for the ride as we show you how God gave John a vision that foretold the future of his church, just as God knew in advance what my reaction would be to conducting this investigation. Prophecy in Revelation proves that God knows everything and has decreed the future—just as we presented in *Unraveling Daniel*.

4

Vision Proof

On April 21, 2022, the Holy Spirit told me that the church was dirty, and it was time to expose the filth so that followers of Jesus would recognize and address it. I welcomed these visions as I received them and felt blessed to be chosen by the Lord to deliver the messages I received and was documenting. However, personally, my life was in a bit of downspin out of frustration because I loved to talk about my investigation results, but the world wasn't interested. What I was being shown was very exciting to me, but apparently not so to others—including those in the church—and this was very disappointing to me. My work for the Lord consumed me and I continued to investigate and write for much of my waking time. Yet, I was disappointed, but I also understood the reluctance of followers of Jesus to want to discuss corruption in the church. What follower of Jesus wants to learn that the Gospel authors were misnamed so that the RCC could take over the APC and grow to a be a powerful entity with nearly a billion supporters and members?

My Catholic friends considered me to be just another Catholic basher, and those in my nondenominational church ignored my visions and once they saw the titles of my books, they rejected them outright without even considering the contents. I really needed someone to talk to who would consider what I was being shown and really try to understand the message.

DECODING REVELATION

I knew the Lord was with me so I continued to pray that the Lord would soften the hearts of those around me. Just then, the Lord stepped in to help. Some "magic" from heaven was about to come into my life that would prove to my lovely wife, Karen, that the visions I receive are from the Holy Spirit and not from the evil that she continued to consider.

Karen had grown up in a Southern Baptist household where churchgoers are taught a message, and nobody questions the validity of the information. Since she was a toddler, she had been told that Matthew wrote the Gospel of Matthew, John Mark wrote the Gospel of Mark, and Luke wrote the Gospel of Luke and the book of Acts. They were always taught this is a fact and the subject of anonymity and questions regarding the actual authorship were never discussed. Like others in the church, she didn't even want to consider the basis behind my investigation conclusions as the contradictory findings didn't sit well with her. She, like others wondered, who am I to contradict years and years of Christian teaching and famous pastors who have for countless years taught the same messages. God has a beautiful way of proving that he is involved, so let me explain how God showed Karen the validity of the messages I had been receiving from the Holy Spirit.

On April 21, 2022, I received the following second vision along with the one previously discussed:

> It is time to step out in faith and sell our home!
> In this vision I also received a picture of the agent that we were to use to sell our house.

Vision Proof

Selling our house was in answer to prayer so let me capture the importance and impact of this vision by taking you back to the beginning. About four years ago we decided it was time to move to Florida because we love the beach and sunshine. We found our home in paradise on earth on a barrier island near the shores of the Atlantic Ocean on the eastern coast of Florida. The home purchase happened fast because we found ourselves in the very beginning of a booming real estate market in Melbourne Beach, Florida, and realized that we needed to jump at an opportunity to purchase a home before we were priced out of the market by quickly rising home values.

Our house was wonderful—except for several nagging issues that we didn't anticipate. When we tried to enjoy our time on the waterfront canal home swarms of little bugs called *"no-see-ums"* ate us alive. They are worse than mosquitoes, because—surprise—you have a hard time seeing them and they loved us. Whenever we were outside by the water, these small, pesty bugs attacked in swarms, and we ended up with bites all over our bodies that turned into welts. There were more issues that plagued us at our "new" home that was built about forty years ago. I am getting on in years and I developed physical limitations that made it very difficult to keep up with the maintenance required for a home on a saltwater canal located only one-third of a mile away from the Atlantic Ocean. In addition, considering that we lived on a canal that had access to the Indian River, we bought our first ever boat. We have owned waterfront homes with boat lifts for the past fifteen years and never had a boat, so it was time to take the plunge. This brought about unexpected anxieties.

DECODING REVELATION

My experience operating boats has been in deepwater lakes. Although the Indian River looked like it was deepwater, it was a shallow body of water with hazards throughout. Navigating the many small islands and shallow water was too much for me—I wanted to get into a boat and tool around mindlessly and not worry about destroying the propeller and boat motor which would cause a big expense. To top it off, getting in and out of our boat lift was a nightmare. I was not used to operating a boat in tight space or shallow water and all this anxiety about the boat operation resulted in the boat sitting unused on the boat lift. We paid a lot of money for a boat that we never used. Next, the insurance costs for the home were getting out of hand; recent minor hurricanes kept driving up the costs of insurance and we realized that if we were hit by a major one, we would end up homeless because our coverage would not allow us to replace the home. We were getting too old to worry about being homeless should we experience one of the frequent major hurricanes that hit Florida. Finally, and very important, most of my time was spent investigating the Bible and writing books containing the results, and I didn't have a comfortable place to read or write in our home.

Both Karen and I prayed to the Lord every day to get rid of our anxieties and let us focus on the beauty of his creation rather than always being busy with home projects and dealing with the everyday frustrations mentioned above. Knowing that we needed to make a change, we visited many open houses looking for just the right place to move to. One open house we attended was at a condo in a complex a few blocks from our home that seemed to answer all our prayers, but the hot real estate market had sellers only accepting cash offers and all our money was tied up in our home. We told the agent that if our home was sold, we'd scoop up that condo in a minute because it checked all our boxes and was in our price range.

A few months later, Karen and I stopped by on our golf cart to walk through a home on the water in a subdivision called Indian Landing, then told the agent, "This house is perfect." She replied, "There are competing offers that will have this home sold for a purchase price much higher than the listing price and besides, *this home isn't for you.*" We spent a few more minutes talking to this very nice agent named Diane, then Karen signed the real estate agent's register book and we left. After another month or two of praying for direction about our home situation and associated anxieties, I woke up that morning of April 21, 2022, with those two visions—the one related to the book of Revelation investigation I am currently working on, and the other one telling me to sell our house with the face of Diane in the vision. How about that for evidence of the power of God—we were to sell our house and we were told who was supposed to sell it for us—the agent who told us that home in Indian Landing *"isn't for you."*

After about four hours of contemplating that first vision and addressing it in this book, I considered the message to sell our home and flashed back to the only other personal vision I had received from the Holy Spirit. About a year earlier, I had woken up with the Holy Spirit telling me to "get into the stock market" but I wasn't trusting that this vision was from the Lord, so I ignored it. Afterward I watched the stock market skyrocket and I kicked myself for not following the Holy Spirit's directions. That might have been the answer to our prayers back then, but I wasn't in tune with it.

DECODING REVELATION

It was now about 7 a.m. that morning of April 21st and that was the time for me to climb back into bed and slowly wake Karen up. That morning would be especially interesting because I was going to tell her that we needed to sell our house. As expected, she didn't react very well—she lay there speechless. Remember. I mentioned that Karen wasn't completely on board with my visions? I'm sure she wanted to say the following to me:

> "Look, we've been married for over thirty years and suddenly the Holy Spirit is talking to you? The stuff you're writing doesn't even verify what I've heard from pastors through the years, and they run the churches, so why should I believe you, your visions, what you're writing, and what you're telling me this morning? How do I know you're not being led by the devil instead of the Holy Spirit?"

For a few minutes she didn't say anything then softly said, "That's interesting, then what?" and that kept the door open for additional discussion without immediately shutting down the prospect of selling our home. In response, I told her, "I don't know what's next because the vision didn't tell me what to do afterward, I was just told to sell our home, and nothing more." We talked for a few minutes about selling our home and laughed at the possibility of being homeless if we sold it, then I told her that, "The agent we saw in Indian Landing will be selling it, her face was in the vision." We refreshed our memories and recalled that her name was "Diane." I ended the discussion by politely reminding her that, "I have been following *every* message that I have received over the previous two years and each one has provided me direction and given me pieces of the puzzles that I needed to solve long-standing Bible issues that the Lord wanted me to address." I followed that up with, "Why wouldn't *we* follow this message too?"

Karen got out of bed and went on her morning bike ride workout. She returned about an hour later and I observed her checking her phone then having a puzzling look on her face, so I asked her, "What do you see?" She responded, "I have a text message from the agent in your vision and the message reads, 'Are you ready to meet to discuss your future plans?' That's weird because I haven't heard from her at all up until this morning." It had been several weeks since we met this agent and out of the blue Karen received a message from the real estate agent who I had a picture of in my vision to help sell our home—a few hours after my vision! Okay, now it's getting real. After reading her text, Karen reminded me of the sermon we had received the day before that taught about Solomon's dream and sometimes you just must recognize that God is talking to you, and you need to follow what you are being told. The evidence that this was from God was piling up in her mind.

It was still early, so after a few more hours, Karen called and put the real estate agent on the speakerphone then told the agent about my vision and how I had been following these messages from the Holy Spirit, then she discussed the sermon the night before and the timing of the agent's text. The agent responded by saying, "The Lord has a plan!" The Lord did have a plan. Three weeks later, as we were closing on the sale of our home with the agent chosen by the Holy Spirit, we received and accepted a full-price offer that also included the sale of our boat that we weren't using. Our prayers had all been answered including obtaining a cushion through a leaseback option of three months . . . you think the Lord had a part in all this? My boat anxieties were eliminated and, not only that, with the leaseback option we had a bit of a cushion to figure out our next step—we were not yet going to be homeless.

Facing an uncertain future, we realized it was time to start looking for a place to live. The day we were to complete the sale of our home by signing papers, the Holy Spirit provided a new listing for a condo at the same location we were ready to purchase one at several months prior. The location of this condo was even better than the condo we previously looked at and wanted to purchase; this home checked all our boxes. The next morning, the same agent we used to sell our home sent us the listing for that condo and scheduled a walk-through. We were mesmerized with the beauty and found that this top floor penthouse unit met *all* our criteria. The condo was steps from the ocean so we could continue our walks at the beach that I used for quiet time in prayer with the Lord. At eight floors up, the no-see-um issue nearly disappeared and allowed us to sit out on the balcony to enjoy the beautiful and mesmerizing sunrises over the ocean and beach, and sunsets over the Indian River and golf course in the evenings. The maintenance and insurance issues mostly disappeared as the interior of the thirteen-year-old condo was in good shape, and we would only need to do some kitchen and dining room remodeling and the sale prices provided enough money to get this work done. About three weeks later, we completed the purchase of the condo that eliminated all our anxieties and answered all our prayers. I even had a great spot in the living room that provided a wonderful view of the ocean to continue my investigations and writing for the Lord.

Based on this, Karen came on board with the work I am doing for the Holy Spirit and became more engaged and interested in hearing what the Lord has been telling me to document. She still questions what I write as she should—anyone writing about scripture and Jesus should be scrutinized by her and everyone else. I hope this example helps you too see how God answers prayers and is intimately involved in every decision *we* make. However, the answer to our prayers wasn't wrapped up in a nice bow and presented as a certain and obvious path forward—it was presented in a vision that required a giant leap of faith. We didn't have to follow the Holy Spirit's guidance, but we did. Afterward I couldn't help but wonder how many of our other prayers were answered in the past that I failed to recognize because I hadn't stepped out in faith and followed them, with a prime example the vision that had told me to get into the stock market that I ignored. It took many turns and bad decisions to get to where I am today, and I'm sure God was disappointed in me more times than not for not following his direction; but, in the end, I am trying to do what I was always intended to do—working for the Holy Spirit and helping others to find their way to follow Jesus. In closing, I encourage you to step out in faith and follow where God is leading you.

5

Theological Stew

WE START OUR VERSE-BY-VERSE analysis of Revelation by first addressing stories of tradition that have tainted the true message of Revelation to hide the beast. Several years ago, I had a band in Corpus Christi, Texas, called Pelican Stew. This band had three members with different talents providing a mix of sound that came together as a pretty good uniform music presentation. We all brought different aspects to the stage, and our combined sound blended just right to soothe the audience's thirst for live music. Pelican Stew did not play original music; we played music that other bands created and perfected, then we added our own personal touch to the music that reflected our talents and personalities. We learned music that other successful bands had played, then rehashed it. We changed the music by giving it our own personal touch, but in general we simply replayed the songs for our audiences.

I titled this chapter "Theological Stew" because I have seen a lot of similarities between playing music and ministers. Like Pelican Stew's rehashed music, preachers and teachers of Jesus seem to regurgitate the same message of Revelation they learned from someone else. Most add a bit of a twist to the message but take away the personal touch, and they are teaching stories that others have created. I emphasize here *"stories that others have created,"* because what I'm referring to is not scripture—these are stories of tradition. A good example of the theological stew of Revelation can be obtained from "Who Wrote Revelation?" by Clarence L. Haynes, Jr., May 28, 2020, at https://www.biblestudytools.com/bible-study/topical-studies/who-wrote-revelation.html where we find:

> The book of Revelation was written around AD 95. Prior to him writing the book, there was a time of tremendous persecution in the church. At this time, the ruling Roman emperor was Domitian. John was persecuted because he was fulfilling his mission, preaching the gospel and making disciples. As part of his persecution, he was exiled to the island of Patmos. He refers to this in the first chapter of Revelation: "I, John, your brother and companion in the suffering and kingdom and patient endurance that are ours in Jesus, was on the island of Patmos because of the word of God and the testimony of Jesus" (Revelation 1:9).
>
> Patmos was a small penal colony to which John was banished. I guess this was the emperor's method of trying to shut him down and silence him. What's interesting to note is that in this place of exile and banishment, God gave him this great revelation. It is just a reminder that your circumstances don't limit God from using you or revealing truth to you. God is greater than your circumstances.

Theological Stew

This theological stew, that has no scriptural or historical confirmation, is uniformly repeated and regurgitated throughout the church. This author even added a little flavor to the story by adding the opinion, "I guess this was the emperor's method of trying to shut him down and silence him." However, in general, whenever you hear the introduction to a series of sermons on Revelation you will hear about John's imprisonment in his nineties when he received this vision. I've heard this story more times than I can count on two hands—just like I repeatedly heard the theological stew of the Gospel authors Matthew, Mark, and Luke. There's just one major problem with this Revelation theological stew, as we will show throughout this rest of this book—it's not true. Like the Gospel-author story, when we look closely at the Revelation theological stew, we see flashing red lights indicating that there are major problems with this tale too.

First, let's examine the words that John wrote—the truth:

> I, John, your brother and companion in the suffering and kingdom and patient endurance that are ours in Jesus, was on the Island of Patmos because of the word. (Revelation 1:9)

There are two immediate conclusions from these introductory words: John is being persecuted and he is preaching the words of Jesus Christ. John specifically ties his distress (in the suffering) to being a companion to those in the church of Jesus Christ (and kingdom) who are being persecuted for their beliefs. John is telling us that suffering and working for the Lord are expected. Acts 8:1 tells us that after the execution of

Stephen, "A great persecution arose against the assembly which was in Jerusalem in that day" and that they "were all scattered abroad throughout the regions of Judea and Samaria, except for the apostles." *All* Christians were being hunted and persecuted after the first recorded execution of one of the men helping to start the church, so John being persecuted was not unusual—it was common knowledge.

Now, let's turn to my Study Bible to look for facts that support the Revelation theological stew. A portion of the summary description for Revelation 1:9 from the NIV states:

> *Patmos:* A small (four by eight miles), rocky island in the Aegean Sea some 50 miles southwest of Ephesus, off the coast of modern Turkey. It probably served as a Roman penal settlement. Eusebius, the "father of church history" (AD 265–340), reports that John was released from Patmos under the emperor Nerva (96–98).

We find out where Patmos is and the characteristics of the geology but look closely and you see a key word *"probably"* associated with the statement that Patmos is a Roman penal settlement. Probably means that the theologians of the NIV believe it is likely, but it isn't certain. The NIV claims the proof for the Patmos story comes from a man named "Eusebius" who lived in AD 265–340 and documented that "John was released from Patmos under the emperor Nerva." That alone raises a red flag because Eusebius provided this documentation about 200 years after John lived. If you follow the trail of Eusebius you will find that he is referring to information from a man named

Theological Stew

Irenaeus estimated by https://earlychristianwritings.com/irenaeus.html to have been written between AD 175 and 185. This documentation is closer to the time of the apostles but still generations separated from eyewitness accounts. We have two men who weren't alive when John lived making a claim without other proof and with no ability for them to witness what they have stated.

I'm sure many of you are saying, "But I believe them because they are early church fathers!" This is where we part company. As an investigator, if I can't connect statements to eyewitnesses, the statements are meaningless. The statements from Eusebius and Irenaeus are not eyewitness statements, therefore, they are not evidence and can't be considered as evidence. Based on this, can we claim that this story is a lie and John was *not* in prison in Patmos at an old age when he wrote Revelation? No, we can't but we are just getting started with the analysis.

For those of you who still claim the words of Eusebius and Irenaeus are indisputable evidence for the theological stew of Patmos and John, I ask you to consider the following scripture:

> Little children, these are the end times. And as you heard that the Antichrist is coming, even now many antichrists have arisen. By this we know that it is the final hour. They went out from us, but they did not belong to us; for if they had belonged to us, they would have continued with us. But they left, that they might be revealed that none of them belong to us. (1 John 2:18–19)

DECODING REVELATION

John and the other disciples are trying to find dedicated Jesus' worshippers to develop into the next generation of church leaders, but they are not at all successful. John says that *"none* of them belong to us"; so, in other words, John is telling the church not to believe the words of those who are taking over the church because they are false teachers.

It wasn't only John who warned about false teachers; Jesus also cautioned the church:

> "Be careful," Jesus said to them, "take heed and beware of the yeast of the Pharisees and Sadducees." (Matthew 16:6)

The Pharisees and the Sadducees were the religious leaders who corrupted the Word of God with rules of men. Jesus knew that these men were not going away after he started his church. They enjoyed prestige, political connections, power, and even financial benefits from their position as Jewish leaders in society. They were not about to give that up for Jesus, so Jesus knew that they would infiltrate and corrupt the church; they would not allow Jesus to replace them.

Peter also warned us about the introduction of crazy stories that would lead those attempting to follow Jesus, astray:

> But false prophets also arose among the people as false teachers will also be among you, who will secretly bring in destructive heresies, denying even the Master who bought them, bringing on themselves swift destruction. (2 Peter 2:1)

Theological Stew

I could go on and add information from other apostles too, but I'll stop here because we have seen enough. We have other clear warnings from God about how false teachers would negatively impact the church of Jesus Christ. Were Eusebius and Irenaeus false teachers? If you read *The Early Church Father Catholic Fraud* and *Unraveling Daniel,* you know that John's statement was true, and a great false church immediately took over the church after the apostles passed on, so based on the timing and impact of their comments, I believe they were part of the RCC false church.

Furthermore, both prophetic books—Daniel *and* Revelation—predict and provide all the dirty details of how the false teachers would take over and corrupt the church. Jesus even provided warnings about the seeds of the corruption that were already sown in the beginning church when he referred to the *"synagogue of Satan"* (Revelation 2:9 and 3:9). Daniel and Revelation both claim that there will be false teachers claiming to speak for God and they will claim the church of Jesus Christ as their own. Based on all these warnings in scripture I don't trust *any* of the tradition injected into the Church to complement scripture. I put all my trust in Jesus and the words of the people he chose to develop the documentation for the church—the Gospel.

Let's next consider the story of John being in prison. It was common for the apostles starting the church to brag about being in prison as though it were a badge of honor. With prompting from the Holy Spirit, I searched scripture for the word *"prison"* and found sixty-one references to it in the New Testament. From scripture we learn about the following prisoners:

DECODING REVELATION

1. John the Baptist was in prison where he was executed (Mark 6:27)
2. A man in prison named Barabbas was traded for the life of Jesus (Luke 23:17–25)
3. The apostles were put into prison (Acts 5:18–25)
4. Saul dragged followers of Jesus off to prison (Acts 8:23)
5. James was in prison (Acts 12:2)
6. Peter was in prison (Acts 12:5)
7. Paul and Silas were together in prison (Acts 16:23)
8. Paul became a prisoner again (Acts 25:14)
9. Paul's associates named Andronicus and Junia are fellow apostles and prisoners (Romans 16:7)
10. Aristarchus, a prisoner with Paul (Colossians 4:10)
11. Epaphras, a prisoner with Paul (Philemon 1:23)

That's an extensive list and my point is that we have the documentation for many prisoners in the New Testament because those starting the church and spreading the words of Jesus are *proud* to claim that they have been put in prison for following Jesus. But John does not mention this badge of honor here, and why not? The only reason can be that he isn't in prison, he is on the Island of Patmos preaching and teaching to the churches that he had helped start. There was a group of men from Asia who were blessed with the Holy Spirit that day of Pentecost (Acts 2:9) and, without a doubt, John was on Patmos to help a group of these men from that region of the world to start and grow the church of Jesus Christ. If John had been in prison at this time, he certainly would have added the few words that would have made this clear.

Theological Stew

Next, let's put the Revelation theological stew to the smell test—does it make sense? We now know that the story of John being in prison doesn't make sense, but what about Jesus providing the revelation to John at an old age—does this make sense? What could be a possible reason for Jesus waiting to give John this Revelation until he is an old man near death? I can't think of one reason, can you? Soon you will see how the first four chapters of Revelation were provided to John to share with the other apostles to help them start the church. John and the other apostles needed this information when they were all alive in the early days of starting the church, not when John was the last apostle alive, and the church has already been completely taken over by false teachers. The only answer that makes sense is that John received this revelation very early in the days of starting the church because the Holy Spirit had guidance to share with the apostles to help them start and grow the church. Revelation was provided to give people hope through the "great tribulation" that the apostles had already seen begin (Revelation 7:14). I addition, if you have already read *Unraveling Daniel*, you understand the beast will infiltrate the church and take it over as soon as the seven-year protected period of the church ends (Daniel 9:24–27 and Revelation 12:6–14).

During our research into that aspect of the theological stew we came across a nugget that proves the dating of Revelation to have been much earlier than when stated by those crafty early church fathers. God left specific breadcrumbs in scripture that confirm without a doubt that the theological stew of Revelation is a created fable with the full intention to support the church of the false teachers—the RCC. We will provide this evidence

in the next chapter when we discuss the letter 2 Peter in relation to the identification of the two witnesses.

In summary, we have a story that tells us John was an old man in a prison on the island of Patmos when he received the prophecy of Revelation in a vision, but the following facts dispute this story:

- There are no eyewitnesses or facts that prove John was an old man and in prison.
- Revelation chapters 2 through 4 are guidance to help start and grow the church, therefore, this vision must have been received by John very early in church history.
- There is no logical reason for God to wait to give this vision to John when he is old and near death—it fails the smell test.
- The words of the disciples are golden, the words of everyone else who came later, such as Eusebius and Irenaeus, are to be rejected:
  - John warned those trying to follow Jesus to not trust the words of anyone but the disciples because false teachers had taken over the church.
  - Jesus warned about the words of false teachers.
  - Peter warned about the words of false teachers.
  - Both Revelation and Daniel prophecy states that false teachers would immediately and completely take over the church after the seven-year protected period of the church starting in AD 26 ended in AD 33 (Daniel 9:24–27 and Revelation 12:6–14)

Theological Stew

With this data in mind can you give me one reason to accept the theological stew that came from two men who never even knew the apostles? Based on the above alone I can't believe the story, but we are not through yet because God provided more evidence. The identification of the two witnesses becomes the motive for the theological stew created by the false teachers that came after the apostles. The next chapter will help prove that this story was created to prevent the world from knowing the identity of the two witnesses, because with their identity known, the RCC loses their reign over the church; Peter loses his designation as the special disciple with authority over the church.

Two Witnesses

*T*HERE IS NO CONSENSUS among Christians about who the two witnesses of Revelation chapter 11 are, and I was quickly overwhelmed at the possibilities presented by various factions of the church. Some suggest that the two witnesses are Moses and Elijah or Enoch and Elijah who will come at the time of the end. Others claim that that Joshua and Zerubbabel or even two unknown prophets will come during another theological stew fable—the seven-year tribulation period that we proved to be untrue in *Unraveling Daniel*. Revelation theological stew generally claims that the two witnesses are prophesied to appear in the final period before Christ returns. One site that swayed from the theological stew pointed me to a documentary called "Unlocking the Mystery of the Two Prophets: Revelation 11," which apparently claims that the founder of the Mormon church and his brother who lived during the nineteenth century were the two witnesses. Surprisingly, I did find one person who concluded that Peter and Paul are the two witnesses. I wasn't sure how he came to this conclusion, so I wrote him an email and never heard back.

This chapter introduces proof for the identification of the two witnesses as Peter and Paul the apostles, and with this introduction, we delve into scripture to find more proof of the dating of the book of Revelation. We will present some more compelling evidence that indicates theology has been tainted to promote the theological stew built to support the hierarchy of the rulers of the RCC. Take away the theological stew to find Peter and Paul as the two witnesses, then as we stated earlier, the RCC loses their claim that Peter is set above the rest of the disciples. Like the Gospel-author story, the answers are buried in scripture as God ensured that there would be enough breadcrumbs to follow the trail to find the truth.

Can we find any historical documentation that proves or even disproves Peter and Paul as the two witnesses? The only reliable documentation about the church is presented in scripture so this is the foundation of our search. We know from our past work that Peter did not write any of the four Gospels, but he did use his faithful friend and brother Silas to document his experiences with Jesus in the Gospel of Luke, the book of Acts, and the letter 1 Peter (see *The Early Church Father Catholic Fraud*). God had a scribe write for Peter so that later in church history we would be able to unravel what we are revealing now when we closely examine the second letter attributed to Peter called 2 Peter.

The introduction of 2 Peter claims that this letter is coming from Peter:

> Simon Peter, a servant and apostle of Jesus Christ, to those who have obtained a like precious faith with us in the righteousness of our God and Savior Jesus Christ: (2 Peter 1:1)

We searched the letter for indication that Silas or another scribe penned this letter for Peter, but we found none. We thought this to be highly unusual, so we first started to look at what others claimed. I went to www.earlychristianwritings.com, to try to find the facts surrounding this letter. This site estimated the dates that Christian documents were written and they provided the range "AD 100–160" but with very little certainty "(2/5)**." This site also had a link to a theologian named Daniel B. Wallace, who wrote on June 24, 2004, "22. Second Peter: Introduction, Argument, and Outline" the following:

> From one perspective, this short epistle is the most disputed book in the NT canon as to authenticity. From another, the issue of authorship is already settled, at least negatively: the apostle Peter did not write the letter. The vast bulk of NT scholars adopts this second perspective without much discussion.

My first quick look at 2 Peter raised a red flag when I saw a reference to Peter in this opening of the letter, "Simon Peter," because this is the same reference used in that fabricated comment written in the Gospel of Matthew that the RCC based their entire existence on (again, see *The Early Church Father Catholic Fraud*):

> Simon Peter answered, "You are the Christ, the Son of the living God." (Matthew 16:16)

References to Peter as Simon Peter are not common outside of John's Gospel where he frequently refers to Peter as "Simon Peter"—seventeen times in total. The usage of *"Simon Peter"* is very rare in other scripture. There are only two mentions of

"Simon Peter" in addition to the 2 Peter 1:1 reference, Matthew 16:16 and Luke 5:8. We proved Matthew 16:16 to be a verse that the RCC added to scripture to build a case for Peter to be the leader of their church (see *The Early Church Father Catholic Fraud*). The reference to "Simon Peter" in Luke 5:8 would have come from Peter, therefore, from this language, we can conclude that either John or Peter contributed to this letter. With this, we move forward considering that the author could be Peter or John.

Initially, when I read and reread 2 Peter, I had indications that Paul penned this letter because of the writing style. Paul had a habit of using run-on sentences with many words to describe behaviors. For example, in Romans 1:28–32, Paul uses twenty-three different terms in one sentence to describe those who refuse God in their lives. There are other examples of this, and when I read the following from 2 Peter, I immediately thought of Paul and his style of writing:

> Yes, and for this very cause adding on your part all diligence, in your faith supply moral excellence; and in moral excellence, knowledge; and in knowledge, self-control; and in self-control, perseverance; and in perseverance, godliness; and in godliness, brotherly affection; and in brotherly affection, love. (2 Peter 1:5–7)

This may seem like Paul's writing, but this is not proof, so I started to dig into the details of the letter to look for more clues. I considered the words in these verses from 2 Peter to be somewhat rare, so I performed a language analysis.

Two Witnesses

We took those rarely used terms mentioned in 2 Peter 1:5–7 with the exception of the word *"knowledge"* that I considered to be somewhat common; *diligence, moral excellence, self-control, perseverance, godliness,* and *brotherly love,* and searched New Testament scripture using www.biblegateway.com and the WEB for their usage. We present the results in the following table:

Word	Total	Paul's Letters	Luke	Paul/Acts¹	Peter/Acts¹	1 Peter	2 Peter	John²
Diligence³	4	3	0	0	0	0	1	0
Moral	2	1	0	0	0	0	1	0
Self-control⁴	11	7	0	1	0	2	1	0
Perseverance⁵	10	5	0	0	0	0	2	3
Godliness	16	11	0	0	1	0	4	0
Brotherly affection	3	0	0	0	0	1	2	0

¹ Sections of Acts attributed to either Peter or Paul (see *The Early Church Father Catholic Fraud*).

² Referenced in the book of Revelation written by John.

³ There are two references to diligence in the book of Hebrews we haven't included.

⁴ The use of self-control *and* self-controlled are addressed.

⁵ The site www.biblegateway.com did not for some reason pick up the word *"perseverance"* in 2 Peter so I added them to the following summary.

- The word *"diligence"* is found exclusively in Paul's letters, 2 Peter, and the book of Hebrews. Paul contributed to this letter, and, in addition, Paul may be the author of Hebrews or contributed to it.
- The word *"moral"* is only used twice; once in Paul's letters and once in 2 Peter. Paul contributed to 2 Peter or is likely the author.
- *"Self-control"* together with *"self-controlled"* are terms exclusively used in scripture by both Peter and Paul. This

indicates that either Peter, Paul, or both contributed to this letter.
- *"Perseverance"* is a word exclusively used by Paul in his letters, John in Revelation, and the author of 2 Peter. This indicates that Paul, John, or both contributed to this letter.
- The word *"godliness"* is exclusively used in scripture by both Peter and Paul, indicating that they both contributed to 2 Peter.
- The term *"brotherly affection"* is exclusively used by only Peter in 1 Peter and, since it is referenced in 2 Peter, it indicates that Peter contributed to the letter.

In conclusion, we have indications from this first step of language analysis that Peter, Paul, and John contributed to or authored the letter 2 Peter in combination. Since the letter 2 Peter reads like a farewell letter and we know that Peter and Paul are targets of imprisonment by the false teachers (Acts 12:5, 16:23, and 25:14) and John is not, based on these results, I consider that 2 Peter might be from the words of Peter and Paul in prison with John as the scribe.

Let's examine a few additional rare words presented in the letter 2 Peter. First, I noticed the word *"corruption"* used in 2 Peter 1:4 that I didn't believe was commonly used by the apostles, so I searched for it and found the following four references to it in the New Testament: Acts 13:34, Galatians 6:8, 2 Peter 1:4, and 2 Peter 2:19. In *The Early Church Father Catholic Fraud*, we determined that Acts 13:34 was in a section of Acts that Silas wrote from Paul's words, therefore, every usage of the word *"corruption"* in the WEB translation is

Two Witnesses

exclusively attributed to Paul. Furthermore, the fact that Paul mentions *corruption* twice in this one letter named 2 Peter indicates that corruption is on his mind as he is writing or contributing to it.

As I read on, I came across another verse that seemed to be from Paul:

> For we didn't follow cunningly devised fables when we made known to you the power and coming of our Lord Jesus Christ, but we were eyewitnesses of this majesty. (2 Peter 1:16)

There are a few very important clues in this verse that provide great insight to the authorship of this letter. I did a search for the apparently rare word *"fable"* and found it to be used only four times in scripture—three times by Paul in his letters and this one reference in 2 Peter. Paul wrote this verse. However, there is another very important word to look at—*"eyewitnesses."* I searched scripture and found only one other reference to it in the WEB—Luke 1:2 and this came from Peter. Paul never once used the word *"eyewitnesses"* or *"eyewitness"* because Paul never claimed to be one of the "eyewitnesses" of Jesus' mission and miracles—this was reserved for Jesus' disciples. This verse, 2 Peter 1:16, appears to have come from both—Peter and Paul.

I went back and reread chapter 1 of 2 Peter and realized I had missed a very important clue: one phrase stuck out like a sore thumb as evidence of Paul's writing:

> I think it right, as long as I am in this tent, to stir you up by reminding you, knowing that the putting off of my tent comes swiftly, even as

our Lord Jesus Christ made clear to me. (2 Peter 1:13–14)

According to Acts 18:3, Paul was a tentmaker. There are only four references in scripture comparing the physical body of a human to a "tent" and we just read two uses of the term in these verses and the other two uses are credited to Paul the tentmaker in 2 Corinthians 5:1–4. There is *no way* that Peter noted the body as a tent—only a tentmaker would do this and that is Paul. Therefore, we can claim with confidence that Paul contributed or wrote 2 Peter.

We are still not through yet as we have more embedded evidence of authorship in 2 Peter:

> For he received from God the Father honor and glory when the voice came to him from the Majestic Glory, "This is my beloved Son, in whom I am well pleased." We heard this voice come out of heaven when we were with him on the holy mountain. (2 Peter 1:17–18)

These verses address the transfiguration of Jesus (Matthew 17:1–8, Mark 9:2–8, and Luke 9:28–36) and we know from that scripture that only the inner circle disciples Peter, John, and James were present on the mountain with Jesus to witness this event. The author of 2 Peter says "*We* heard this voice come out of heaven" indicating that at least two of those who were transfiguration eyewitnesses are contributing to this letter. We know from Acts 12:2 that James was killed early in church history, therefore, this letter must have Peter and John contributing to it.

Two Witnesses

As I was about to wrap up this review, the Holy Spirit ensured that I wouldn't miss one more important clue:

> We have the more sure word of prophecy; and you do well that you heed it, as to a lamp shining in a dark place, until the day dawns. And the morning star arises in your hearts: knowing this first, that no prophecy of scripture is of private interpretation. For no prophecy ever came by the will of man: but holy men of God spoke, being moved by the Holy Spirit. (2 Peter 1:19–21)

Wow—we just stumbled across numerous breadcrumbs—thank you Jesus! Let me explain! There are only three references to the specific term *"morning star"* in the New Testament—the reference in this verse and two references to it in Revelation, verses 2:28 and 22:16. Both references to the *"morning star"* were descriptions that came to John from Jesus through an angel. Scripture has just verified that this letter came *after* John received the vision he documented in Revelation, *and* either John is contributing to the letter or Peter and Paul have had access to John's book of Revelation that in Revelation referred to Jesus as the *"morning star."* This entire verse references Revelation (*lamp, morning star,* and *prophecy*), therefore, John is certainly with Peter and Paul as this farewell letter is being written.

We have now confirmed through analysis of the language in 2 Peter that three of the apostles Peter, Paul, and John contributed to the contents. But why is this important? First, it puts Peter, Paul, and John together at a troubled time in the church. The letter 2 Peter, reeks of doom—you can feel it and sense it as you go through it. In fact, this letter seems as though it is the final letter from apostles who have received a death sentence. Paul makes it clear in 2 Peter 1:13–14 that he will be losing his tent soon. The next verses tell the complete story—everything you need to know about this letter:

> But false prophets also arose among the people, as false teachers will also be among you, who will secretly bring in destructive heresies, denying even the Master who bought them, bringing on themselves swift destruction. Many will follow their immoral ways, and as a result, the way of the truth will be maligned. (2 Peter 2:1–2)

Can the message of 2 Peter be clearer? There are factions currently in the church (false prophets also arose among the people) and they will not go away—they will remain in the church (as false teachers will also be among you). Those who are persecuting Paul and Peter will covertly be sabotaging the church with their tradition (who will secretly bring in destructive heresies). These false teachers will corrupt the church by rejecting Jesus (denying even the Master who bought them). The false teachers will be popular and successful (Many will follow their immoral ways) and they will corrupt the Word of God and the church of Jesus Christ (and as a result, the way of the truth will be maligned).

I hope you read that last passage and understood it because these three apostles have just told you that false teachers will stop at nothing to feed their flesh—they will even corrupt scripture and provide theological stew that will hide their deceit!

Two Witnesses

Look at how they corrupted this letter to support Peter as the leader of the church by assigning it as being authored by only Peter, and how they twisted the meaning of Revelation with a heresy that was created to support them. In closing, I believe there a few additional references to Revelation in this letter. For example:

> With eyes full of adultery, they never stop sinning; they seduce the unstable; they are experts in greed—an accursed brood! (2 Peter 2:14)

This appears to be a reference to the "great prostitute" and enticing maddening wine of the woman discussed in Revelation who represents what will become of the pure church of Jesus Christ—the beast (Revelation 17:5 and 18:3 among many other verses). There is another very important 2 Peter reference to Revelation we present next:

> But do not forget this one thing, dear friends: With the Lord a day is like a thousand years, and a thousand years are like a day. (2 Peter 2:8)

Revelation 8:1 told us that one hour of heaven time is equal to 2,300 years of earth time—eternity never ends and those who corrupt the church will face a punishment that is just for their actions.

In 2 Peter we have a letter from three apostles who together were facing death. As you will see later when we analyze the section of the two witnesses presented in Revelation chapter 11, there are two witnesses who will extend Jesus' sacrifice for the Jews to the Gentiles. These two witnesses are representatives

DECODING REVELATION

of Jesus and that means they must have been appointed by God to extend the mission of Jesus (Matthew 28:18–20); in doing so, Peter and Paul preached the Word of God, performed healing miracles (e.g., Acts 3:6–8 for Peter and Acts 14:9–11 for Paul), and raised people from the dead (e.g., Acts 9:40 for Peter and Acts 20:9–12 for Paul). Only Paul and Peter satisfy these requirements. Why is John with Peter and Paul? We can't be sure, but we do know that he will be witnessing the sacrifice of the two witnesses, and it will make John's "stomach sour" (Revelation 10:9–10).

In closing, why is this chapter important to understand Revelation? Revelation captures the entire future of the church and predicts the takeover of the church by a group of false teachers we know from history is the RCC. The RCC stopped at nothing to control the Word of God and use it for their benefit. Their actions included presenting theological stew such as the Gospel-author story and the fables we have seen written and promoted as the truth about Revelation. With John living to an old age in prison and receiving the Revelation vision, Peter and Paul cannot be the two witnesses and John cannot have witnessed them being executed because the two witnesses are prophesied as coming in the distant future during a mysterious seven-year period created from Daniel 9:24–27. John, with Peter and Paul as the two witnesses who are sacrificed, fulfills prophecy and completes the sacrifice of Jesus extension to the Gentiles.

I challenge you to find evidence of the deaths of Peter and Paul—you won't, because it doesn't exist anymore. Imagine how much written documentation that must have been written about Peter and Paul as they faced execution, then rose from

Two Witnesses

the dead, caused the destruction of Rome by breathing fire on it, then ascended into heaven. This was not a secret, and we can all be assured that many followers of Jesus wrote about it. However, their documentation was replaced with the heresy Peter, Paul, and John warned you about in 2 Peter and other documentation from them that remains in the Bible. The false teachers secretly brought in their destructive heresies. Peter and Paul, the two witnesses who faced execution, managed to get a letter out to the church—likely through John who warned that after they perished the church would be taken over by corrupt false teachers. You will see more evidence of this as we go verse-by-verse through chapters 10 and 11 of Revelation. There is only one answer—the two witnesses *are* Peter and Paul.

However, the theological stew created by the false teachers who took over the church continues to hide their corruption and fraud by strategically pointing the church to future corruption through the tradition that they've embedded in scripture. Jesus warned the disciples of what would happen to them:

> But watch yourselves, for they will deliver you up to councils. You will be beaten in synagogues. You will stand before rulers and kings for my sake, for a testimony to them. The Good News must first be preached to all the nations. (Mark 13:9–10)

In that same section of scripture, Jesus later added a few very important words:

> Most certainly I say to you, this generation will not pass away until all these things happen.

DECODING REVELATION

> Heaven and earth will pass away, but my words will not pass away. (Mark 13:30–31)

This whole section of scripture Mark 13:1–31 has addressed the lives of the disciples who will face persecution and death from false teachers as they document the words and actions of Jesus and start the church. Did these false teachers leave the church after they killed the apostles? Of course not, they grew in power as prophesied in Daniel and, as you will soon see, also prophesied in Revelation.

Theological stew has been provided to the church to hide the truth of corruption in the church by pointing the church to the distant future. The disciples, "this generation," witness everything in those verses of Mark while they are alive and it's not a comfortable story. As a side note, Jesus just confirmed the dating of the Gospels to be during the protected period of starting the church specified in Daniel 9:27—the last half of the seven-year mission of Jesus (You will be beaten in synagogues . . . The Good News *must first* be preached to the nations). With visions reminding them of everything the Lord did and said, they were "helped" to document the Gospels between AD 30 and AD 33. Afterward, the persecution of the apostles started.

7

Jesus and the Scribe

WE TURN NOW TO the verse-by-verse analysis of Revelation. The book of Revelation starts out with John, the disciple of Jesus, telling us that he is receiving this prophecy, and explaining why he is receiving it. Note in the title of this chapter that we called John a *"scribe"* and not an author. John is a scribe because he did not come up with or create the contents of the information presented in the book of Revelation, he merely wrote down what Jesus instructed an angel to tell John to write. I used the word *"merely"* tongue in cheek because what a privilege it was for John to have Jesus select him to write down the message that Jesus wanted documented for *all* of history to be delivered to *all* people.

The first verse provides very important messages:

> The revelation from Jesus Christ, which God gave him to show his servants what must soon take place. He made it known by sending his angel to his servant John, who testifies to everything he saw—that is, the word of God and the testimony of Jesus Christ. (Revelation 1:1–2)

Initially, Jesus tells (The revelation from Jesus Christ) John (which God gave him) that this revelation has been provided to John to present to the disciples (to show his servants) what will happen to the church in the future (what must soon take place). Is it a leap to call the disciples Jesus' "servants"? Not if you read John 18:36 where Jesus says, "If my kingdom were of this world, then my servants would fight, that I wouldn't be delivered to the Jews." As we go through Revelation you will see that *"must soon takes place"* is a reference to the entire future of the church being provided in context through the clock in heaven. From our review of the book of Daniel we found that Revelation 8:1 in combination with Revelation chapter 20 explained that an hour of heaven time is equal to 2,300 years, and this prophecy that John observes will cover the entire future of the church from the start to the end. Just as we saw in the book of Daniel prophecy, and in heaven time, 2,300 years is *"what must soon take place."* Next, we learn that John is working for the Lord to fulfill the commission he received (Matthew 28:19–20) to start the church (John, who testifies to everything he saw). John, one of Jesus' twelve servants, had an assigned job to document the story of Jesus (Mark 13:9 and 13:30) to help start the church (that is, the Word of God and the testimony of Jesus Christ).

John has already written his Gospel and now this revelation will be an addition to that. Like the Gospel of John, this revelation will be the "word of God and the testimony of Jesus Christ." If you have a Bible like mine, the words of Jesus have been printed in red ink, but here in Revelation they are mistaken in their sporadic use of red ink—John is saying that *this whole book* should be in red ink because the Lord is delivering this message through an angel (He made it known by sending his angel). This entire revelation that John received is the Word of God through an angel Jesus sent to John.

Jesus and the Scribe

Since, John has written down the "word of God" and the "testimony of Jesus Christ," this prophecy must have a very important message for you and all other people of the world:

> Blessed is the one who reads aloud the words of this prophecy, and blessed are those who hear and take to heart what is written in it, because the time is near. (Revelation 1:3)

This passage is a very important key to this revelation. First, Jesus tells the leaders of the church that their job is to read this prophecy (blessed is the one who reads aloud the words of this prophecy) to whoever they encounter (and blessed are those who hear). The followers of Jesus are *expected* to understand this prophecy (and take to heart). The key word I highlighted in that last passage was *and* because it takes two actions to be blessed; we must listen (hear), *and* in response we must act on these words (take to heart what is written in it). Revelation was not intended to be a mystery—it was intended to be *understood* by the church.

The last part of that verse tells us why it is so important to be blessed with the message of salvation in Revelation—"because the time is near." And what time is near? The answer is easy—soon *"your tent"* as the apostle Paul called your body, will collapse and you will either head in one direction to be with Jesus or head to the opposite direction for eternal damnation with a punishment that never ends. If an hour in heaven is equal to 2,300 years, your death is coming up in minutes because one hundred years of earth time is like one-twenty-third of an hour of heaven and that means that one hundred years is less than

DECODING REVELATION

three minutes in heaven. Your time is passing away quickly, and Jesus is warning you to pay attention to his words so that you find and follow him prior to your time running out. Once you die, your eternal destination is determined and there can be no change.

Next and right up front, John is told that the message of this revelation is *all* about the church:

> John, To the seven churches in the province of Asia: Grace and peace to you from him who is, and who was, and who is to come, and from the seven spirits before his throne, and from Jesus Christ who is the faithful witness, the firstborn from the dead, and the ruler of the kings of the earth. To him who loves us and has freed us from our sins by his blood, and has made us to be a kingdom and priests to serve his God and Father—to him be glory and power for ever and ever! Amen. (Revelation 1:4–6)

The Lord told me in my visions that the book of Revelation is all about the church, but did I really need a vision to figure this out? Not if I had understood John's vision here. According to www.biblegateway.com a great resource for searching the Bible, there are eighty-one references to the number *"seven"* in the New Testament and nearly half of these, thirty-six, are in the book of Revelation. Some of these are:

1. The seven churches (Revelation 1:4)
2. Seven spirits before the throne of Jesus (Revelation 1:4)
3. Seven golden lampstands (Revelation 1:12)

Jesus and the Scribe

4. Seven stars (Revelation 1:16)
5. Seven lamps (Revelation 4:5)
6. A scroll with seven seals (Revelation 5:1)
7. Seven horns and seven eyes which are the seven spirits of God (Revelation 5:6)
8. Seven angels with seven trumpets (Revelation 8:2)
9. Seven thunders (Revelation 10:3)
10. Seven signs (Revelation 12:1)
11. Seven crowns (Revelation 12:3)
12. Seven plagues represented by seven bowls of wrath (Revelation 15:6–7)
13. Seven hills (Revelation 17:9)
14. Seven kings (Revelation 17:10)

Whenever *"seven"* is specified in scripture, we know that we are being presented something that is complete and final—nothing can be added to it or taken away. Daniel 9:24–27 presented Jesus as the *seven sevens* who is the most complete person who ever lived—he is God. In that prophecy of the "seventy sevens," Jesus was described as having a seven-year mission to preach, teach, become the sacrifice for the removal and forgiveness of all sin, rise from the dead, and start his church. The most complete person ever who we know is Jesus, had a "seven"-year mission that would be a complete and permanent decree of forgiveness for the sins of mankind. This prophecy, together with the book of Revelation and additional scripture references in Daniel, accurately predicted the year that Jesus would arrive, his mission, and how he would set up his church. It was the complete story of Jesus, the Son of God, as a man.

DECODING REVELATION

In our passage above, we see that Jesus is going to tell John the complete message about the church. John is familiar with these seven churches of Asia because in AD 30 he started those churches with men who were filled with the Holy Spirit on Pentecost day (Acts 2:9). Using the concept of the meaning of seven from prophecy and looking at verses 1:4–5 again, we learn that this message from Jesus is:

- addressing the entire apostolic church (To the seven churches);
- is coming from God (Grace and peace to you from him who is, and who is to come) through his angels (seven spirits before his throne) and God's son (and from Jesus Christ who is the faithful witness);
- it will be about the promise of resurrection (the firstborn from the dead) coming from Jesus who was the first to come back from the dead; and,
- that makes Jesus the King of kings (and the ruler of the kings of the earth).

We who are blessed will achieve our salvation through Jesus (has freed us from our sins by his blood) and we are to serve him in his church (and has made us to be a kingdom and priests to serve his God and Father).

Note that there is a reference to *only one* church (*a* kingdom). All these various branches of Christianity we see today are not in accordance with what Jesus wanted! Having denominations of the church of Jesus Christ each with their own operating manual and specific format is not following the Word of God, it is evidence of a corrupted church! There is only one church of

Jesus and the Scribe

Jesus Christ and there should be no factions or groups calling themselves "certain" or "special" Christians because they are the *only* ones with the knowledge of the kingdom of Jesus. The disciples started *one* church—the APC—and that is what Jesus commanded the church to be—one congregation reading the one message about Jesus from one source—*the apostles.*

The church was designed to have numerous individual churches that make up the one church—like each of the seven churches of Asia, but there is only the one church of Jesus Christ. Every church branch is to be the same. As you will see in chapter 4 of Revelation all church branches are to have the same worship service, the same focus, and led by an elder of the church that will watch over and ensure the flock is following only Jesus. In addition to that prophecy in Revelation, the following documentation from the apostle Paul is just a small sampling of scripture supporting the one church:

> He is the head of the body, the assembly, who is the beginning, the firstborn from the dead; that in all things he might have the preeminence. (Colossians 1:18)

> For in one Spirit were we all baptized into one body, whether Jews or Greeks, whether bond or free; and were all made to drink into one Spirit. (1 Corinthians 12:13)

> He put all things in subjection under his feet, and gave him to be head over all things for the assembly which is his body, the fullness of him who fill all in all. (Ephesians 1:22–23)

John also let us know that Jesus stated that there is only one complete church:

> I have other sheep, which are not from this fold. I must bring them also, and they will hear my voice. They will become one flock with one shepherd. (John 10:16)

The passages above are all singular; Jesus is the head of the church and the body of the church. There is only one church of God—the church of Jesus Christ, and all followers of Jesus are the body of the church. The church of Jesus is clearly a seven—complete in every way. Jesus alone is the head of this one church—the firstborn and the ruler of the kings of the earth. There will be one church and one shepherd—the APC started by the apostles with Jesus as the shepherd (They will become one flock with one shepherd).

Next, there are important details in the vision that John observes:

> "Look, he is coming with the clouds," and "every eye will see him, even those who pierced him," and all peoples on earth "will mourn because of him." So shall it be! Amen. (Revelation 1:7)

Is this a reference to *all* people seeing Jesus at one specific appearance, or is this a reference to the majesty of God that is apparent throughout creation—especially when we look up at the clouds? If you consider that everyone who lives during the New Covenant of Jesus will exist in an "hour" of time in heaven, then this could appear as though it is one continuous stream of followers of Jesus. We also have the following as guidance:

> "Most certainly I tell you, he who hears my word and believes him who sent me has eternal life, and doesn't come into judgment, but has passed out of death into life." (John 5:24)

There are two groups of people—those who believe in Jesus and those who don't. From John 5:24 we just learned that both groups will see Jesus when they die. Those who "believe him who sent me has eternal life" will see Jesus on his throne in heaven. Those who don't believe will "come into judgment" and will see Jesus to be judged and condemned. Jesus will make his presence known to everyone (every eye will see him), including those who persecuted him (even those who pierced him), but not everyone will hear his voice and be called home because they rejected the sacrifice of Jesus (and all peoples on earth "will mourn"). God has decreed the process of salvation through Jesus (because of him) and there will be no changes to it (So shall it be! Amen). Note that Jesus has referred to those who reject him as *"peoples on earth."* This concept is very important as we move forward through Revelation.

Next, we find that Revelation 1:8 reaffirms that Jesus is, was, and always will be God. Then, John provides readers some background into his vision:

> I, John, your brother and companion in the suffering and kingdom and patient endurance that are ours in Jesus, was on the island of Patmos

DECODING REVELATION

because of the word of God and the testimony of Jesus. (Revelation 1:9)

The author describes himself as John, but how do we know that this is John the disciple? First, we only learn of three Johns in scripture: John the Baptist, John the disciple of Jesus, and John also called Mark, who is mentioned only a few times in scripture. We know that John the Baptist had been executed many years prior to this Revelation and John also called Mark is not a prominent person in the church, so these two Johns cannot be the author. The only author that makes sense is the John who claimed to be the disciple "whom Jesus loved" (John 13:23, et al.) and the disciple who confidently claims that he is "John, your brother and companion." This person must be the disciple of Jesus who also wrote the Gospel of John and a few other letters recorded in the New Testament. We've already thoroughly addressed the theological stew presented by corrupt theologians many years ago intended to falsely point the message of Revelation to address the *distant* future rather than the *total* future of the church. John will be obtaining chronological accounts of the *total* future of the church.

Next, there is a command from Jesus sounding like a trumpet:

> On the Lord's day I was in the Spirit, and I heard behind me a loud voice like a trumpet, which said, "Write on a scroll what you see and send it to the seven churches to Ephesus, Smyrna, Pergamum, Thyatira, Sardis, Philadelphia, and Laodicea." (Revelation 1:10–11)

Jesus and the Scribe

John is with Jesus (in the Spirit) on the "Lord's day" and what does this mean? We can't say for sure because neither the WEB nor NIV present another instance of the "Lord's day." We can say that John is being moved by the Holy Spirit when he hears a command from Jesus to write down things that Jesus will show him about what is going on in the churches that John is familiar with. Jesus wants the message to the churches to be official, documented forever, without confusion or questioning by the recipients, and read by the church so he commands John to write it on a scroll. The message is to apply to the total church (send it to the seven churches) but specifically it will address the churches John is familiar with.

The churches the disciples are starting will be *the only* place for the light of Jesus to emanate from and spread:

> I turned around to see the voice that was speaking to me. And when I turned I saw seven golden lampstands (Revelation 1:12)

Jesus stated that he was the light of the world and that the disciples would follow in Jesus' footsteps and be an extension of Jesus to spread the light (Matthew 5:14). John turned around to see the voice of someone and saw "seven golden lampstands" that we know from Revelation 1:20 is the entire church.

John turns to see who is speaking to him:

> and among the lampstands was someone like a son of man, dressed in a robe down to his feet and with a golden sash around his chest. The hair on his head was white like wool, as white as snow, and his eyes were blazing fire. His feet

were like bronze glowing in a furnace, and his voice was like the sound of rushing waters. In his right hand he held seven stars and coming out of his mouth was a sharp, double-edged sword. His face was like the sun shining in all its brilliance. (Revelation 1:13–16)

John sees someone that looks like Jesus standing amidst the church (and among the lampstands was someone like a son of man). Since we will learn in Revelation 1:20 that a star is an angel assigned to a church, this man can only be Jesus because all the angels are in his right hand (In his right hand he held seven stars). In addition, we know that this is Jesus because he rides out on the white horse with a double-edged sword and only Jesus does this (Revelation 19:11–17). The church is all about Jesus and Jesus has all the authority over the light of the world (His face was like the sun shining in all its brilliance).

John was overcome with emotions and fell at the feet of Jesus who comforts John (Revelation 1:17) and gives John a message:

> I am the Living One; I was dead, and now look,
> I am alive for ever and ever! And I hold the keys
> of death and Hades. (Revelation 1:18)

Jesus was executed but now lives (I am the Living One; I was dead, and now look, I am alive) and Jesus will live forever (I am alive for ever and ever!). Hades must be hell because Revelation 6:8 tells us that it closely follows death. Jesus is life and if you are with him, you will find life, but without Jesus you will find permanent death and eternal damnation in hell (And I hold the keys of death and Hades). As we presented above, all who

Jesus and the Scribe

believe in Jesus have eternal life and all others will die—Jesus holds the keys to eternal life and death. But what about Matthew 16:18–19 that claims that Jesus gave these keys to Peter? If Jesus gave Peter the keys to life and death, why wouldn't Jesus mention that here in Revelation in addition to that one verse in Matthew? Matthew 16:18–19 is clearly a statement that will impact the entire future of the church. Revelation has just verified as true the evidence we found in *The Early Church Father Catholic Fraud* that Matthew 16:18–19 was the work of false teachers who were intent on stealing the church. This claim in one verse was added by false teachers to support their church takeover. As you will soon see, Revelation verifies that the RCC will stop at nothing to take over the church and it will succeed.

John immediately went to work after that Pentecost day when people received the Holy Spirit. He met with those in the crowd from Asia and then, with their assistance, started the seven church branches mentioned in Revelation 1:11. In this vision John has been taken up to heaven to witness how the church needs to spread the light of Jesus so that those who follow Jesus will live, in addition to the grim future for those who reject Jesus—Jesus has the keys. John is a fisherman who, like the other disciples, has the great responsibility to start and commission the church. Jesus commissioned the eleven to start up a church (then added Paul to make it twelve) that will bring millions, and maybe even billions, of people to faith in Jesus. These fishermen are overwhelmed so Jesus is providing them much needed direction and guidance—they are not alone.

The church commission has just been described, and now Jesus will provide the details of the future, starting with what is currently happening in the church:

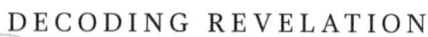

> Write, therefore, what you have seen, what is now and what will take place later. (Revelation 1:19)

With the scope of the church already presented, Jesus wants John to document what he has already seen happening in the church (Write, therefore, what you have seen). Since John is human, his understanding of what is happening in the church is limited. Therefore, Jesus, who sees everything, will help John to understand everything that is going on in the church (what is now). Afterward, Jesus will describe the future of the church for John to document (and what will take place later). Next Jesus provided important details to help the church understand the message:

> The mystery of the seven stars that you saw in my right hand and of the seven golden lampstands is this: The seven stars are the angels of the seven churches, and the seven lampstands are the seven churches. (Revelation 1:20)

The message will be entirely about the church that will spread the light of Jesus throughout the world. John will be getting the complete and total assessment of the condition of the church and how it will grow and change in the future. The disciples will spread the good news of Jesus throughout the church, but they need to be aware of the evil presence that is threatening the church's existence and the true message of Jesus. Jesus tells John how much the church means to Jesus (in my right hand) and that he has assigned angels to help the disciples spread the

Jesus and the Scribe

light of Jesus (seven lampstands) throughout the entire church (seven churches).

Next Jesus will provide John a performance review of the church that will include some of what John has seen but other things that only Jesus is aware of because he is watching everything that is happening in the church.

8

Guidance for the Church

PERFORMANCE REVIEWS ARE PROVIDED by management to help employees improve over time. The disciples have been tasked with starting the church and this includes writing the operating manual—scripture in the form of the Gospels and letters that will provide the management structure and job descriptions for the church. Jesus' goal in the next few chapters is to help the disciples recognize problems in the church that they are to address in their documentation, oversight, and training of new leadership. Remember earlier when we discussed the timing of the Gospels and considered if there was any reason God would wait to give John this revelation? Try to conceive of a reason why God would wait to have the apostles document the words of Jesus and for John to document his Revelation visions. That scenario just doesn't make sense. The disciples need the information in the Gospels and Revelation at the beginning of the church to start, develop, and grow the church through the spreading of the words of Jesus.

Like any good performance evaluation, Jesus will discuss both the good and the bad performance in the church. Jesus will also provide warnings to repent from the bad performance which is also called *"sin."* The warning includes threats of God pouring out his wrath on those church branches and members who do not repent and stop sinning. God will not tolerate sin and he clearly lets the people of the church know that there is no place for sin in the church and he will punish those who are sinning—even with physical harm. The aspect of physical punishment for sinning came as a surprise to me. I have in the past wondered if God physically punishes people for following evil, but I don't need to wonder any more. God's warnings for physical punishment to address sin is crystal clear. Finally, Jesus provides the churches encouragement by reminding them of their reward if they choose to follow Jesus.

Daniel was told that there are angels helping God in the spiritual battle between good and evil (Daniel 10:20–11:1) and John receives the same message:

> "To the angel of the church in Ephesus write: These are the words of him who holds the seven stars in his right hand and walks among the seven golden lampstands. (Revelation 2:1)

We learned earlier that there are angels helping each church and this angel is dedicated to help the church in Ephesus. The angels are working for Jesus (These are the words of him who holds the seven stars). I had a decision of whether to go through each of the seven churches documented in Revelation 2:2–3:22 individually or to summarize the data. I chose the summary route, therefore, we will not analyze each verse in this performance review separately.

In summary, we have the following categories and details:

1. The presence of evil in the church:

Guidance for the Church

- They have lost and left behind their love of Jesus (Ephesus)
- A group of liars, called the "Synagogue of Satan," claim to follow Jesus, but they lie and bring evil into the church—including persecuting followers of Jesus (Smyrna, Philadelphia)
- Pretending to follow Jesus, but they are spiritually dead (Sardis)
- Lukewarm for Jesus—neither hot nor cold (Laodicea)
- Worshiping idols (Pergamum, Thyatira)
- Practicing and promoting sexual immorality (Pergamum, Thyatira)
- Focusing on personal wealth (Laodicea)
- In the city of Satan (Pergamum)

2. Warnings for churches that follow evil rather than Jesus:
- Remove the church (Ephesus, Laodicea)
- Face the sword of Jesus (Pergamum)
- Punishment including sickness and death for themselves and the ones they love (Thyatira. Laodicea)
- Jesus will come like a thief in the night to steal their life (Sardis)
- They will be humbled and judged (Philadelphia)

3. Evidence of Jesus in the church:
- Hard work, perseverance, and spiritual growth in Jesus (Ephesus, Thyatira)
- Not tolerating wicked people (Ephesus)
- Giving preachers the "false teacher test" (Ephesus)

- Enduring hardships and even death for the name of Jesus (Ephesus, Pergamum)
- Hating pagan worship (Ephesus)
- Rejecting those welcoming evil into the church (Thyatira)
- No denying of Jesus (Philadelphia)

4. Blessings for following Jesus:
- Wearing the crown of victory and having eternal life in the kingdom of God (Ephesus, Smyrna, Pergamum, Thyatira, Sardis, Philadelphia, Laodicea)

Note that each of the seven churches is mentioned in categories 1 and 2—no branch of the church is unaffected by evil. If Jesus completed a performance review of the church today, he would find aspects of evil in every church branch in existence. Also note that there is only one blessing specified for following the good of Jesus—wearing the crown of eternal salvation! Nothing else is necessary!

Next in our analysis, we highlight a few specific verses and messages from these two chapters that require more discussion:

1. A "Ten-Day" Trial:

> Do not be afraid about what you are about to suffer. I tell you, the devil will put some of you in prison to test you, and you will suffer persecution for *ten* days. Be faithful, even to the point of death, and I will give you life as your victor's crown. (Revelation 2:10)

Guidance for the Church

I highlighted *"ten days"* because it seemed like an unusual and specific message that I needed to look deeper into. As we have done in the past, we turn to prophecy to help us understand this passage and we find it in Daniel:

> "Please test your servants for ten days: Give us nothing but vegetables to eat and water to drink. Then compare our appearance with that of the young men who eat the royal food, and treat your servants in accordance with what you see." (Daniel 1:12–13)

Seven is complete, therefore, if this test were for seven days it would be the end and complete test. Those in the church will be temporarily tested (suffer persecution for ten days) and if they remain faithful and loyal to Jesus they will be rewarded (I will give you life as your victor's crown). This is a temporary test with a permanent reward.

2. "Come like a thief":

> Remember, therefore, what you have received and heard; hold fast, and repent. But if you do not wake up, I will come like a thief, and you will not know at what time I will come to you. (Revelation 3:3)

Jesus cautions that our first step to find and follow him is to stick to the words written about Jesus and change (hold fast, and repent). If we do not take this step (But if you do not wake up) our temporary test while we live on earth will end with our permanent and eternal death (I will come like a thief) that will come unexpectedly (and you will not know at what time I will come to you). As specified in the fourth seal (Revelation 6:8), death for those who reject Jesus is followed closely by a trip to hell. Reject Jesus and in an instant your future is determined, and it is not a good one.

3. "Inhabitants of the Earth":

> Since you have kept my command to endure patiently, I will also keep you from the hour of trial that is going to come on the world to test the inhabitants of the earth. (Revelation 3:10)

Those who are on trial are judged, and during the hour of the New Covenant time of Jesus, those who reject Jesus, the "inhabitants of the earth," will face trial. If you follow Jesus, you will not be judged:

> He who believes in him is not judged. He who doesn't believe has been judged already, because he has not believed in the name of the one and only Son of God. (John 3:18)

We know that all it takes is belief in Jesus to be welcomed into the eternal church, therefore, those who believe are told to "endure patiently" because their reward is coming. The "hour of trial," the 2,300 years of the New Covenant of Jesus, will see the judgment and condemnation of all who reject Jesus—the "inhabitants of the earth."

Guidance for the Church

4. "Suffering":

> I have given her time to repent of her immorality, but she is unwilling. So I will cast her on a bed of suffering, and I will make those who commit adultery with her suffer intensely, unless they repent of her ways. I will strike her children dead. (Revelation 2:21–23)

Several years ago, a friend of mine who was going through a very difficult time asked me, "Does God punish people for doing bad things?" I fumbled around for words because I really didn't know the answer. I gave my friend a lame answer and bad advice because I didn't know better. I said, "God wants people to repent and change what they were doing, but I don't think he punishes people for their sins." I couldn't have been more wrong as I would have seen if I had thoroughly studied Revelation years before:

> Those whom I love I rebuke and discipline. So
> be earnest and repent. (Revelation 3:19)

There is one common theme in these verses—"repent." Jesus will inflict pain on you and your household to get you to recognize your sin and repent of it. If that doesn't work, then he might just give up on you and pay you a visit like a thief in the night (Revelation 3:3). Revelation is very clear; God will punish people to get them to repent for their sin and change their ways to follow the light of the world—Jesus. If you do not "wake up" and change your ways (repent), the Lord knows your heart and knows when there is no hope for you to repent. If the Lord sees this in you, he has warned you that he "will come like a thief" and it will be too late.

5. "Synagogue of Evil"

For Smyrna (Revelation 2:9), Pergamum (Revelation 2:13), Thyatira (Revelation 2:24–25), and Philadelphia (Revelation 3:9), we see a mention of the presence of Satan in the church—an evil presence within the church:

> I know about the slander of those who say they are Jews and are not but are a synagogue of Satan. Do not be afraid of what you are about to suffer. (Revelation 2:9)

> I know where you live—where Satan has his throne. Yet you remain true to my name. You did not renounce your faith in me, not even in the days of Antipas, my faithful witness, who was put to death in your city—where Satan lives. (Revelation 2:13)

> Now I say to the rest of you in Thyatira, to you who do not hold to her teaching and have not learned Satan's so-called deep secrets, "I will not impose any other burden on you, except to hold on to what you have until I come." (Revelation 2:24–25)

> I will make those who are of the synagogue of Satan, who claim to be Jews though they are not,

Guidance for the Church

> but are liars—I will make them come and fall down at your feet and acknowledge that I have loved you. (Revelation 3:9)

Satan is fully established in most of the church and surrounding locale early in church history. How do we know this is early in church history? Because there is a mention of only one martyr at these churches—it is still rare and special (Revelation 2:13). As the church matures and Satan gets a firm hold on the entire church, martyrs for their faith will become more common. Was this the first martyr for their faith in following Jesus? We can't be sure, but we can date Revelation as being received by John *after* AD 33—when the protection period of the church start-up ended (Daniel 9:27 and Revelation 12:14).

In closing, Jesus promises the church one thing—that if you follow his command, you will have eternal life in the kingdom of heaven. This is no frivolous promise. Jesus will either visit you like the thief in the night when you least expect him and then hell will follow close behind with weeping and gnashing of teeth, or he will call you home for peace and joy in his eternal kingdom. The choice is yours to make. Remember, an hour in heaven is equal to 2,300 years on earth. As we presented in the last book *Unraveling Daniel* an hour of punishment in hell will be like 20 million hours on earth. Can you tolerate the pain and agony you face if you reject Jesus? The decision you make should be thought out very carefully.

What Must Take Place

JESUS HAS TOLD JOHN all the details about what is happening in the church and now Jesus will provide John the last part of that introduction, the "what will take place later" from Revelation 1:19. Jesus has just shown the disciple John the status of the church and as we learned some in the church are sharing the good news of Jesus, but there are also others corrupting the church. The fishermen that Jesus selected to start the church have been provided help by the Holy Spirit and they have been doing the best that they can to share the good of Jesus with others. Jesus will now provide more assistance—he will show John and the rest of the church leaders what he wants the church to look like.

Like a typical performance review, a plan for improving performance will be presented and discussed at the end. Jesus will now provide John and the disciples some specific guidelines he wants implemented in the church:

> After this I looked, and there before me was a door standing open in heaven. And the voice I had first heard speaking to me like a trumpet said, "Come up here, and I will show you what must take place after this." (Revelation 4:1)

DECODING REVELATION

The performance appraisal that Jesus just gave the church was a mixed bag—there were some highlights of great things people were doing to follow Jesus, but evil was present and growing in the church. Right from the start the church was infiltrated by Satan and Jesus is about to provide guidance to counter this effect—he will show John and the disciples what the church is to look like. First, the church is to be the gateway to heaven (After this I looked, and there before me was a door standing open in heaven). Jesus commands (speaking to me like a trumpet) that the apostles are to implement some changes in the church (show you what *must* take place after this). John is told that the church *must* implement the changes that have been decreed by God.

God has all authority over the church:

> At once I was in the Spirit, and there before me was a throne in heaven with someone sitting on it. And the one who sat there had the appearance of jasper and ruby. A rainbow that shone like an emerald encircled the throne. (Revelation 4:2–3)

John physically remains on the island of Patmos, but his Spirit is escorted to heaven (At once I was in the Spirit) where he witnesses Jesus on the throne. Jesus is not alone:

> Surrounding the throne were twenty-four other thrones, and seated on them were twenty-four elders. They were dressed in white and had crowns of gold. (Revelation 4:4)

What Must Take Place

Jesus does not need help in *heaven* to rule, therefore, this *must* be a representation of the church on earth; the church is the bridge to heaven and Jesus is showing John how this bridge will look. There are to be rulers over the church in the church (Surrounding the throne were twenty-four thrones) named elders who report to Jesus (and seated on them were twenty-four elders). The twenty-four elders represent both covenants with God—twelve are for the twelve tribes who followed the law, and twelve are for the disciples who followed Jesus. We know that the apostles followed this guidance because these leaders of the church appointed elders to rule over each new branch of the church:

> When they had appointed elders for them in every assembly, and had prayed with fasting, they commended them to the Lord, on whom they had believed. (Acts 14:23)

> I left you in Crete for this reason, that you would set in order the things that were lacking and appoint elders in every city, as I directed you. (Titus 1:5)

This is good evidence for the book of Acts to have been written *after* John received the Revelation. The church hierarchy became the leaders of the church, the elders the disciples appointed, and the church members referred to in the WEB as the assembly:

> Then it seemed good to the apostles and the elders, with the whole assembly, to choose men

out of their company, and send them to Antioch with Paul and Barnabas: Judas called Barsabbas, and Silas, chief men among the brothers. (Acts 15:22)

They wrote these things by their hand: "The apostles, the elders, and the brothers, to the brothers who are of the Gentiles in Antioch, Syria, and Cilicia: greetings. (Acts 15:23)

The apostles did as they were commanded by the Lord and assigned leaders called "elders" at each assembly or branch of the church.

John observes the power of the church emanating from the throne of Jesus:

> From the throne came flashes of lightning, rumblings and peals of thunder. In front of the throne, seven lamps were blazing. These are the seven spirits of God. (Revelation 4:5)

There is a reference to only one throne here so that must be the throne of Jesus. All power, guidance, and commands come from Jesus (From the throne came flashes of lightning, rumblings and peals of thunder) through the elders to spread the light of the world through the church (In front of the throne, seven lamps were blazing). Jesus wants John to see how the light of Jesus will be spread throughout the world. The church will consist of many branches just as with the tree of life, and each branch will have an elder assigned to be in charge. Every

What Must Take Place

branch of the church is to be the total and complete representation of Jesus to the world (These are the seven spirits of God).

This next verse is very important and feeds into the previous message:

> Also in front of the throne there was what looked like a sea of glass, clear as crystal. (Revelation 4:6)

When we try to figure out what John is saying when he describes this vision to us, we turn in his Gospel to where John quoted Jesus as saying:

> He who believes in me, as the scripture has said, from within him will flow rivers of living water. (John 7:38)

Jesus is the living water. The living water flows from the throne of Jesus and creates the sea—the total assembly of God on earth—the church! There is to be no confusion in the church, and it is to be a peaceful sea of glass, clear as crystal.

The next verse tells us about the feedback loop of the elders:

> In the center, around the throne were four living creatures, and they were covered with eyes, in front and in back. The first living creature was like a lion, the second was like an ox, the third had a face of a man, the fourth was like a flying eagle. Each of the four living creatures had six wings and was covered with eyes all around. (Revelation 4:6–8)

DECODING REVELATION

Nothing in the church will be hidden from Jesus. The four living creatures see everything (they were covered with eyes), are like Jesus (was like a lion), are powerful (like an ox), live among the people (had a face of a man), and are majestically moving around (like a flying eagle). Jesus is God, so what else is like Jesus that sees and knows everything and roams around at will, but the Holy Spirit? The creatures must be a representation of the Holy Spirit. Nothing can take place in the church that will escape the scrutiny of the Lord as he rules over the church through the elders with the assistance of the Holy Spirit. The Holy Spirit will be working with Jesus to observe and hear everything that goes on in the church, then the rumblings, lightning, and thunder are the feedback loop—Jesus is not going to let the church operate in a vacuum. The ongoing spiritual battle for the souls of people has been described. The church is in for a battle.

Everything in the church is to be about Jesus and only Jesus:

> Whenever the living creatures give glory, honor and thanks to him who sits on the throne and who lives for ever and ever, the twenty-four elders fall down before him who sits on the throne and worship him who lives for ever and ever. (Revelation 4:9–10)

Everything that is heard and observed in the church is to be about the worship of Jesus (the living creatures give glory, honor and thanks to him who sits on the throne and lives for ever and ever). The elders of the church are to radiate the church with their obedience and praise of Jesus (the twenty-four

What Must Take Place

elders fall down before him who sits on the throne and lives for ever and ever). John hears the praise of the elders as they "fall down before him who sits on the throne"—they humble themselves before Jesus and their entire existence is for worshiping the majesty of Jesus, their God. The elders are special men who dedicate their entire life to the worship of Jesus. Worship and worshippers in the church are to be 100% dedicated to Jesus and not to the leaders of the church or any other documentation (Revelation 4:11).

In summary, thus far we have seen Jesus describe the church operation and management structure. We know from the book of Acts that the disciples received this message, verbally taught and shared their documentation of the words of Jesus, then assigned elders over the church to represent Jesus to the people of the world through the church. The church is decreed to be an assembly of Jesus with the Holy Spirit interacting daily with the people in the church, then reporting back to Jesus the status of the church. Then, Jesus will provide feedback. I want to close this chapter by emphasizing that there is no confusion in the Word of God and this warning is for church leaders—don't use confusion in the Word of God as an excuse to form your own church worship process and procedures. The church is to be only about Jesus and nothing else and since Jesus is everywhere in the church and sees everything that is taking place—nothing escapes the scrutiny of the Lord. For all you false teachers who think you are getting away with something, your rewards on earth are recognized as corruption of the church and you will be punished for your selfish behavior!

How's that for an opening to a book that is all about the church. As the vision of John proceeds, he will obtain and

document details about what will happen to the church. Next up is a presentation of the reward for those who strive to follow Jesus through the church, written on a scroll that only Jesus can read as the description of the church continues.

Success of the Church

Starting the church was a monumental task for the eleven remaining disciples who would soon be joined by Paul to get the number back to twelve. Jesus didn't want people with experience starting a new business or organization, his only requirement was that he wanted full dedication and devotion to his word. Jesus ascended into heaven but before he left, he promised the disciples that he would provide them guidance through the Holy Spirit:

> I have said these things to you while still living with you. But the Counselor, the Holy Spirit, who the Father will send in my name, will teach you all things, and will remind you of all that I have said to you. (John 14:25–26)

The living water of Jesus was to flow to the church through the disciples through the elders of the church to the assembly. We read in John 14:25–26 that Jesus promised that the Holy Spirit will be with the disciples to help them develop and grow the church. We learn from this passage that the Holy Spirit will also "remind" the disciples of what Jesus said and did so that they can accurately document the Gospels. The disciples were told that their documentation would cover everything the church needs (will teach you all things). Nothing will be left out of scripture—it will be complete because the Holy Spirit is involved in its writing.

John continued to receive guidance on the management and mission of the church written on a scroll:

> Then I saw in the right hand of him who sat on the throne a scroll with writing on both sides and sealed with seven seals. (Revelation 5:1)

The future of the church has been decreed by God—set in stone and written on a sealed scroll. The *entire future* of the church has been written on this scroll because the scroll is full (writing on both sides) and completely sealed (sealed with seven seals). Also, the scroll is held in the right hand of God, therefore, the contents are the Word of God and cannot be altered or changed; the future of the church is the truth of God that has been decreed.

John sees this scroll, but is initially disappointed:

> And I saw a mighty angel proclaiming in a loud voice, "Who is worthy to break the seals and open the scroll?" But no one in heaven or on the earth or under the earth could open the scroll or even look inside it. (Revelation 5:2–3)

At first, it appears as though nobody will be able to open and read the scroll but then there is the victory of Jesus and the hope for all people:

> Then one of the elders said to me, "Do not weep! See, the Lion of the tribe of Judah, the Root of

Success of the Church

> David, has triumphed. He is able to open the scroll and its seven seals." (Revelation 5:5)

John is grieved because the Word of God for the church is contained on the scroll, but it appears as though nobody will be able to open and read it. An elder informs John of the truth indicating that the elders are to only speak words coming from Jesus and nothing else. Only Jesus is able to communicate the Word of God to the church and the elders are to share it (no one in heaven or on the earth or under the earth could open the scroll or even look inside it). There is an important reference to the devil—"under the earth." Satan will inject his words into the church, but they are not the Word of God—only Jesus' words are to be shared in the church by the elders.

John is provided the details of why Jesus is the only one able to read the Word of God:

> Then I saw a Lamb, looking as if it had been slain, standing at the center of the throne, encircled by the four living creatures and the elders. The Lamb had seven horns and seven eyes, which are the seven spirits of God sent out into all the earth. (Revelation 5:6)

Jesus is the sacrifice (Lamb) who was killed for the sin of all people, but he didn't stay dead—he rose from the grave (looking as if it had been slain) and now Jesus is ruling over the church (standing at the center of the throne). Jesus with the help of the Holy Spirit (encircled by the four living creatures) is the boss of the leaders of the church (and elders). Jesus who was the sacrifice for sin (The Lamb) has the complete power and

authority of God (seven horns), can see everything (and seven eyes), and is the representation of God (are the seven spirits of God) to all the people of the world (sent out into all the earth).

Jesus takes the scroll out of God's hand because he alone is worthy:

> He went and took the scroll from the right hand of him who sat on the throne. And when he had taken it, the four living creatures and the twenty-four elders fell down before the Lamb. Each one had a harp and they were holding golden bowls full of incense, which are the prayers of God's people. (Revelation 5:7–8)

John has just seen Jesus standing at the throne, and now he sees Jesus taking the scroll from the hand of God who was sitting on the throne (right hand of him who sat on the throne). The sacrifice of Jesus allowed him to take the scroll from God's hand and, because of this, the church with the presence of the Holy Spirit in it, will worship him (the four living creatures and the twenty-four elders fell down before the Lamb). The leaders of the church are to be leading the church in the worship of Jesus (Each one had a harp), and are the conduit for the prayers of the assembly (golden bowls full of incense, which are the prayers of God's people). Take note that these prayers *are* the golden bowls full of incense because they *are* accepted by Jesus because later you will read how insincere prayers from the church make their way to the throne of Jesus and these prayers will be rejected (Revelation 8:3–4). Also take note that

Success of the Church

the elders are hand delivering the prayers of God's people (they were holding golden bowls full of incense).

The sincere prayers acknowledge that the assembly is all about the worship of Jesus:

> And they sang a new song, saying: "You are worthy to take the scroll and to open its seals, because you were slain, and with your blood you purchased for God persons from every tribe and language and people and nation. You have made them to be a kingdom of priests to serve our God, and they will reign on the earth. (Revelation 5:9–10)

All worship in the church is to be for Jesus and about his sin sacrifice. There is only one church (You have made them to be a kingdom) with elders assigned by Jesus to rule throughout the earth:

> Then I looked and heard the voice of many angels, numbering thousands upon thousands, and ten thousand times ten thousand. They encircled the throne and the living creatures and the elders. (Revelation 5:11)

The church will be successful in its mission to save people from their sin through the blood of Jesus. The numbers of saved souls that "encircled the throne" is countless—thousands upon thousands in addition to a hundred million (10,000 x 10,000 = 100,000,000). Jesus shows John that the church elders will successfully lead the assembly to receive their reward to be with

Jesus at the time of the end. Those whose sincere prayers were delivered by dedicated elders of the church will live with Jesus and surround the throne.

The multitude of saved souls break out in praise and worship (Revelation 5:12–13), then chapter 5 ends with the following verse:

> The four living creatures said, "Amen." And the elders fell down and worshiped. (Revelation 5:14)

The word *"Amen"* is used to signify the ending of a prayer to God. Jesus provided the operating guidance and management directives for the church, and it will successfully help many to accept the blood of Jesus as the sacrifice that frees them from sin and gives them life in the presence of Jesus and God forever. The importance of ending chapter 5 with the word *"Amen"* signifies that you have just seen a glimpse of what eternity with Jesus in his kingdom will look like. The one holding the future of the church in his right hand, Jesus, was crucified as the sacrifice for the world, then rose from the dead to reign over his church. The elders of the church will lead people to praise and worship only Jesus. The multitudes of those who have accepted this saving grace provided free from Jesus are surrounding the throne and worshiping Jesus.

What a beautiful story, but that is not the full picture of the church. Although many will be saved through the church of Jesus Christ, there will be turmoil in the church. God decreed free will for his creation of people and this will result in the rejection of Jesus to follow evil. The two-sided scroll will contain

Success of the Church

all the details of the battle between good and evil for the soul of every person. Jesus is about to unseal the future of the church and the details will be shocking unless you have taken to heart how 1 John written by John and 2 Peter written by Peter, Paul, and John captured their broken hearts when they witness the corruption that is infiltrating and taking over the church as they faced death for Jesus. With this closing, we turn to the contents of the scroll as Jesus opens the seals and reads from the scroll. The accuracy of the predictions will shock you so hold on to your seat as we proceed.

The Church Future

THE FUTURE OF THE church has been decreed—all the details were documented in advance. What was written in Daniel summarized the decree of the church of Jesus Christ and Revelation will verify the prophecy from Daniel and expand on some of it. The scroll is protected with seven seals, meaning that it is authentic and will contain the complete future of the church. The first four seals are different than the last three—they represent what the Holy Spirit witnesses during this period of the church. Jesus will start the church, but then the synagogue of Satan that Jesus described earlier, is prophesied to grow in strength, power, and appeal to completely take over the church of Jesus Christ.

Jesus opens the first seal:

> I watched as the Lamb opened the first of the seven seals. Then I heard one of the four living creatures say in a voice like thunder, "Come!" I looked, and there before me was a white horse. Its rider held a bow, and he was given a crown, and he rode out as a conqueror bent on conquest. (Revelation 6:1–2)

Jesus, the rider on a white horse, was crowned a king (given a crown) to save the world from sin (he rode out as a conqueror bent on conquest). This is the first phase of the church—the purity and gift of Jesus that was present on the day of Jesus' sin sacrifice.

The first seal revealed life, purity, and conquest, but the next seal reveals death and destruction:

> When the Lamb opened the second seal, I heard the second living creature say, "Come!" Then another horse came out, a fiery red one. Its rider was given power to take peace from the earth and to make people kill each other. To him was given a large sword. (Revelation 6:3–4)

John witnesses another horse and rider but this one represents evil and sin (Then another horse came out, a fiery red one). How do we know it's evil and sin? Because we know that Jesus went to earth to provide peace to all through his sacrifice—those who accept Jesus will have peace in heaven for eternity (John 14:7). However, those who oppose Jesus will remove his peace from the earth (Matthew 10:34). This evil entity in the church will cause many to sin by removing Jesus from the church (given power to take peace from the earth) and sin will bring death through persecutions and executions (and to make people kill each other).

How soon after the coming of Jesus did evil enter the church? We know from the performance appraisal Jesus provided the church that the synagogue of the Satan was already present. Therefore, we can assume that as soon as the sacrifice of Jesus was complete Satan was present to destroy the church. Satan tried to destroy Jesus at birth, then tried to destroy the mission of Jesus but he couldn't because God protected Jesus and the disciples for seven years. The church started with the peace of Jesus, then we know John and the other apostles wrote about the evil effects of false teachers. Jesus tells John that this evil entity will be prominent, powerful, and effective (To him was given a large sword). Also, note that this is one organized entity because the large sword was given to "*him*"—singular. The devil is on the move and since the second seal does not have a fraction associated with it like seals four through six that describe a portion of the church being affected by evil, the devil will make an impact throughout the church.

The directions are clear, and the disciples will follow Jesus' decree. The elders are assigned to oversee the church on earth and John and the disciples have been putting people in charge of the church who are not worthy, so I can only imagine just how bad John, Peter, Paul, and the rest of the disciples felt when they wrote their letters. If you remember the parable of the weeds that Jesus spoke of, the synagogue of Satan is the weed that will sprout up in the church and grow (Matthew 13:24–30). You can tell John is heartbroken when he wrote about the false teachers and corruption of the men they assigned as the future elders of the churches (1 John 2:18–19). The despair was also present in the letter 2 Peter as the false teachers are preparing to execute disciples.

The church was immediately contaminated with corrupt false teachers and the synagogue of Satan will grow and flourish. Jesus opens the third seal and again the Holy Spirit (living creature) orders John to pay close attention:

> When the Lamb opened the third seal, I heard the third living creature say, "Come!" I looked, and there before me was a black horse! Its rider was holding a pair of scales in his hand. Then I heard what sounded like a voice among the four living creatures saying, "Two pounds of wheat for a day's wages, and six pounds of barley for a day's wages, and do not damage the oil and the wine!" (Revelation 6:5–6)

The voice among the four living creatures indicates that this seal affects the *entire* church. The message appears to be one about nutrition and in general it is. We get the following explanation from the NIV Study Bible for these verses:

> One quart of wheat would be enough for only one person. Three quarts of the less nutritious barley would be barely enough for a small family.

A person can survive off this amount of nutrition, but someone is working all day just to survive. But this message is not about physical nutrition, it is about *spiritual* nutrition as it applies to the church. Jesus is the light and eternal life, therefore, the black horse *must* be representing death. Jesus provides a gift of salvation —the nourishment that brings eternal life (John 6:35 and numerous other passages), but there will be an evil presence in the church that will take away the gift of salvation and replace it with work requirements.

The synagogue of Satan will demand that people in the church will work to remove their sin, however, there is no amount of work that will bring about the forgiveness of sin. As

The Church Future

I read this description, I thought of the RCC requirements of going to a priest to confess sins then receiving a work requirement in the form of penance that they say will remove the stain of the confessed sin. But that is only one example of a book full of work requirements created by the RCC (*Catechism of the Catholic Church*). Object to work requirements or reject any of the many *Catechism*'s requirements and the church can remove a person from the church they call the "one true church of Jesus Christ."

Next Jesus opens the fourth seal and the Holy Spirit calls John over to observe one final horse—a pale one:

> When the Lamb opened the fourth seal, I heard the voice of the fourth living creature say, "Come!" I looked, and there before me was a pale horse! Its rider was named Death, and Hades was following close behind him. They were given power over a fourth of the earth to kill by sword, famine and plague, and by the wild beasts of the earth. (Revelation 6:7–8)

The definition of *Hades* can be obtained from Luke 16:23 that presents the story of the rich man begging for relief from the torture of Hades. Hades must be hell and from Revelation 6:7–8 we find that this horse is named "Death" and hell is "following close behind." The pale horse symbolizes the sickness and death that the work requirements of the third seal will bring to the church. Not only will the beast of the RCC starve those seeking to follow Jesus, in their quest to spread their false church they will join with governments to control nearly a fourth of civilization and will kill many as they continue to expand (They were given power over a fourth of the earth to kill by sword, famine, and plague, and by the wild beasts of the earth).

Once the creatures have completed the presentation of the description of the four seals, Jesus will open two seals that present the damaging effects of this period of reign over the church by the RCC:

> When he opened the fifth seal, I saw under the altar the souls of those who had been slain because of the word of God and the testimony they had maintained. They called out in a loud voice, "How long, Sovereign Lord, holy and true, until you judge the inhabitants of the earth and avenge our blood?" Then each of them was given a white robe, and they were told to wait a little longer, until the full number of the fellow servants, their brothers and sisters, were killed just as they had been. (Revelation 6:9–11)

The fifth seal tells us that there is a decreed length of time for the RCC to control the church through the persecution of followers of Jesus. The souls are described as being "under the altar" and when you visualize an altar and the space under it, you don't think of numerous souls. John does not specify how many souls are under the altar, but we can guess from other scripture that this is still early in church history. Two of these souls under the altar are likely Stephen that we read about in the book of Acts who was stoned to death for following Jesus

The Church Future

soon after the start of the church (Acts 6:8–7:60) and Antipas who was martyred at the church of Pergamum (Revelation 2:13). John's brother James is not mentioned here, therefore, this might indicate that John received this vision early in church history shortly after the protection of the apostles starting the church ended in AD 33 and before AD 42 when James was executed (Acts 12:2). We also learn from these verses that the people being slain are those in the church who are rejecting the words of the RCC that make them work for their salvation described in the third and fourth seals, so they are executed for following the words of Jesus (those who had been slain because of the word of God and the testimony they had maintained).

Those who were executed for their faith call out in a loud voice for vengeance for their deaths. The "inhabitants of the earth" are doing the killing and when the set number of martyrs is reached, the souls of the martyrs will be avenged and those in the RCC persecuting them will be judged. In heaven time it will be less than an hour "until the full number of the fellow servants, their brothers and sisters, were killed just as they had been." The martyrs are "servants" of the Lord who have been washed clean of their sin through their faith in the words of Jesus (each of them was given a white robe). When the total number of martyrs for the Lord has been reached at the end of the RCC's reign in AD 1330 (see *Unraveling Daniel*), the inhabitants of the earth will be judged (until you judge the inhabitants of the earth and avenge our blood).

Next, we learn that the reign of the RCC over the church is prophesied to be very successful—there will be a period of great persecution coming to the church:

> I watched as he opened the sixth seal. There was a great earthquake. The sun turned black like sackcloth made of goat hair, and the whole moon turned blood red, and the stars in the sky fell to earth, as figs drop from a fig tree when shaken by a strong wind. The heavens receded like a scroll being rolled up, and every mountain and island was removed from its place. (Revelation 6:12–14)

The sixth seal is a message of darkness, death, and destruction that will be experienced in the church as the RCC tightens their grip. Jesus will be completely removed from the church—the light will be removed from the world (The sun turned black; the stars in the sky fell to earth). The RCC beast has been turned loose to destroy the church (There was a great earthquake) and it will be very successful at spreading the darkness of evil.

We know that the *mountains* represent the presence of God; Moses received the Ten Commandments on a mountain (Exodus 24:12–18), Jesus gave his sermon on the mount (Matthew 5:1–7:29), Jesus chose his twelve disciples while on a mountain (Luke 6:12–16), and Jesus was also transfigured on a mountain where he met Moses and Elijah (Luke 9:28–36). Psalm 125 is a perfect example of scripture comparing the Lord's presence to a mountain:

> Those who trust in Yahweh are as Mount Zion, which can't be moved, but remains forever. As the mountains surround Jerusalem, so Yahweh

The Church Future

surrounds his people from this time forward and forever more. (Psalm 125:1–2)

A mountain signifies the power and great presence of Jesus and the Word of God, and God is all-powerful and working among his people. Eventually, the truth of Jesus will not be found anywhere in the church (the heavens receded like a scroll being rolled up)—the RCC will completely replace the words of Jesus with their words making the church work for their salvation (and every mountain and island was removed from its place).

Those stealing the church will attempt to hide in the words of Jesus:

> Then the kings of the earth, the princes, the generals, the rich, the mighty, and everyone else, both slave and free, hid in the caves and among the rocks of the mountains. They called to the mountains, "Fall on us and hide us from the face of him who sits on the throne and from the wrath of the Lamb. For the great day of their wrath has come, and who can withstand it?" (Revelation 6:15–16)

The great false church will consist of people from all aspects of society (the kings of the earth, the princes, the generals, the rich, the mighty, and everyone else, both slave and free) who are pretending to follow Jesus (hid in the caves and among the rocks of the mountains). But the deception of the false teachers is not fooling God because the Holy Spirit is everywhere in the church watching. At the end of the reign of the RCC, God will start to pour his wrath out on them for their arrogance and disobedience (They called to the mountains, "Fall on us and hide us from the face of him who sits on the throne and from the wrath of the Lamb."). The false teachers who stole the church will be punished (For the great day of their wrath has come).

The Transition and Seventh Seal

WE HAVE BEEN THROUGH the first six seals that have addressed time through the reign of the RCC. In summary we have learned the following:

1. The first seal represented the coming of Jesus who arrived in the world to conqueror sin. This is the seventy sevens of Daniel 9:24–27 that we thoroughly discussed in the previous book addressing prophecy, *Unraveling Daniel* (5/6 BC–AD 30). The Messiah's mission culminated with the execution sacrifice of Jesus in AD 30.
2. The second seal represents the devil who first tried to prevent Jesus from completing his mission. This is a reference to the seven of Jesus (Daniel 9:24–27). Although Satan attempted to sabotage and destroy Jesus and the church before it took hold, God protected Jesus and the disciples during this entire time (Revelation 12:6 and 12:14). But the seeds of evil were planted in the early church as the "synagogue of Satan" (Revelation chapters 2 and 3).
3. The third seal represents the takeover of the church by the RCC that started immediately as the church protection was lifted and the devil was allowed to persecute

and execute those starting the church in AD 33. The "synagogue of Satan" grew into the beast of the RCC that removed the gift of salvation and implemented their process of work requirements to remove the stain of sin.

4. The fourth seal represents the period of the reign of the RCC that lasted from AD 30 to 1330 as they formed agreements with governments to expand while persecuting and executing those who resisted their reign. This is the bronze kingdom as represented in the statue vision of Nebuchadnezzar (Daniel 2:39), the beasts that will attack the church (Daniel 7:2–8), and the goat that attacked the Old and New Covenants of God (Daniel 8:5–7). John receives and presents many more details of the beast known as the "RCC."

5. The fifth seal reveals that there will be a set time decreed for the false teachers to take over the church and, during this time, they will be executing followers of Jesus that reject their work requirements. Those that have been martyred for their commitment to Jesus seek vengeance for their spilled blood and they are told it will happen when the set number, 144,000 from all the tribes of Israel, "were killed just as they had been."

6. The sixth seal captures the effects of the church takeover by the false teachers. The church of Jesus Christ is essentially out of operation while the RCC reigns over the church. The RCC has removed Jesus, the light of the world, from the earth.

The Holy Spirit has completed describing a portion of the seals that summarizes the entire length of time we call the reign

The Transition and Seventh Seal

of the RCC—the prophesied beast. A brief review of historical records will verify that the first six seals have already occurred—the church was completely controlled by false teachers who claimed they spoke for God and made their words equal to scripture. The reign of the RCC is decreed to end when Jesus returns to rule with the set number of martyrs who are executed for their dedication to Jesus; this is described in the seventh seal (Revelation 8:1), but before we get to this, we have a whole chapter of scripture in Revelation to address those that gave their lives for faith in Jesus.

At the end of the reign of the RCC we learn of a transition:

> After this I saw four angels standing at the four corners of the earth, holding back the four winds of the earth to prevent any wind from blowing on the land or on the sea or on any tree. Then I saw another angel coming up from the east, having the seal of the living God. He called out in a loud voice to the four angels who had been given power to harm the land and the sea: "Do not harm the land and the sea or the trees until we put a seal on the foreheads of the servants of our God." Then I heard the number of those who were sealed: 144,000 from all the tribes of Israel. (Revelation 7:1–4)

Four angels are preventing the wind (holding back the four winds) of the Holy Spirit from blowing on the church during the reign of the RCC. The Holy Spirit is not affecting the world (the earth), the church (the sea), or the elders (the trees), because the evil presence of Satan through the free will of men is controlling the church. At the end of the reign of the RCC, this will change when an angel (Then I saw another angel) from God (coming from the east) with a message of Jesus (having the seal of the living God) releases the Holy Spirit to bring the wrath of God down on the corrupt church (harm the land and the sea and the tree) once the set number of followers of Jesus are executed for their faith (the number who were sealed: 144,000 from all the tribes of Israel). The RCC's control over the church will end and the reign of Jesus will begin.

You might have just brushed over a key point in this last verse—the "servants of our God"—the servants of God were, who we discussed earlier, dedicated followers of Jesus (Revelation 1:1–2). Revelation 14:4–5 will tell us that the 144,000 are those who rejected the teachings of the RCC to follow Jesus and were killed for it. We ended verse Revelation 7:4 with the exact number of martyrs for their faith, then the next four verses tell John that each tribe of Israel will contribute equally to the martyrs (Revelation 7:5–8). Is 144,000 an exact number of martyrs who died for their faith during the reign of the RCC? In *Unraveling Daniel,* we found the numbers in prophecy to be exact; so, we conclude that, "Yes, there were 144,000 martyrs who were killed for their faith in Jesus prior to the change that ushered in the reign of Jesus."

There is one more key point in that last section of scripture that needs to be addressed prior to moving on—the seal on the foreheads of the servants of God. Will there be an actual physical seal on the foreheads of the people of God? The answer to that question is an obvious, "No, because these 144,000 people are dead and dead people don't have bodies—their bodies are

The Transition and Seventh Seal

gone—unless the seal is on their new body." But let's look at it another way through the following passage from the disciple John who wrote this scripture:

> Jesus answered them, "Most assuredly I tell you, you seek me, not because you saw signs, but because you ate of the loaves, and were filled. Don't work for the food which perishes, but for the food which remains to eternal life, which the Son of Man will give to you. For the Father, even God, has sealed him." (John 6:26–27)

God sealed Jesus as the giver of life. Was Jesus walking around with a visible seal of approval on his forehead provided by God? Certainly not. Has God put a visible seal on your forehead if you are a follower of Jesus? Certainly not. Has God put a mark on your head or wrist? No! Before we leave that scripture from John, you can't help but wonder if Jesus just warned us all about what was revealed by the third seal (Don't work for the food which perishes).

John knew that these souls were sealed by God because they were under the altar—there just wasn't the set number yet. Look at Revelation 3:12 when Jesus tells John, "I will also write on them my new name." Those who follow Jesus will be renewed with the name of Jesus written on them. Is Jesus going around with a pen writing his name on people? I hear of Christians watching out for and claiming that something is the mark of the beast, but like the seal of God, the mark of the beast will be on your heart and not something physical that others can see. Remember, Jesus sees and knows everything.

DECODING REVELATION

You don't need a physical seal—he can see what's in your heart and knows whether you've received his seal, or the seal of evil referred to later as the *"666"* (Revelation 13:18).

Even though the RCC controlled the church with work requirements, many will still be saved through belief in Jesus:

> After this I looked, and there before me was a great multitude that no one could count, from every nation, tribe, people and language, standing before the throne and before the Lamb. They were wearing white robes and were holding palm branches in their hands. And they cried out in a loud voice: "Salvation belongs to our God, who sits on the throne, and to the Lamb." (Revelation 7:9–10)

It's great to see that the number of followers of Jesus saved during the time of the RCC reign (wearing white robes and holding palm branches) are so many that John could not count them (a great multitude that no one could count) and they came from every part of the world (from every nation, tribe, people and language):

> Then one of the elders asked me, "These in white robes—who are they, and where did they come from?" I answered, "Sir, you know." And he said, "These are they who have come out of the great tribulation; they have washed their robes and made them white in the blood of the Lamb." (Revelation 7:13–14)

The Transition and Seventh Seal

First, who is the person who asks John the question? It's one of the twenty-four elders that represent the church of Jesus. I always wondered why John wrote that the elder asked him that question, but the answer is clear to me now. One of the elders, a leader of the church, asks John if he knows where all these people came from, and John tells him it's a stupid question because an elder will know—all those who came to know and find Jesus were saved by hearing elders preach about Jesus. Even though the RCC will reign over the church for many years, and it seems like the elder's work is worthless, Jesus is showing John just how important the work of the elders is. The men and women teaching the truth of Jesus will still reach a multitude of people who will be saved during this long period of strife in the church (they who have come out of the great tribulation).

For those of you who are waiting for the "great tribulation" to come, you missed it. Jesus has told John that the "great tribulation" occurred during the reign of the RCC and this is easy to see and believe from historical records. The 144,000 men and women leaders of the church were martyred for their faith in Jesus and the RCC reigned with an iron fist over the church for 1,300 years from AD 30 to 1330. If you've read *Unraveling Daniel* you know that a man named John Wycliffe, who would translate the Bible for all to read to free the Word of God, was born in AD 1330. Scripture was scrubbed to ensure the reign of RCC could not be challenged and people were kept from hearing the words of Jesus—every aspect of the church was filtered through the RCC. Read the *Edict of Thessalonica* to see how the RCC and the Roman government worked to replace Jesus with their false church. Even though 144,000 martyrs of Jesus might not seem like a lot over a 1,300-year period, many others were killed who wanted no part of Jesus but also wanted no part of the RCC; the 144,000 is just the number of martyrs for Jesus. Many others were persecuted during the RCC reign and that is why it is called the *"great tribulation,"* a time of great hardship in the church.

The final verses in chapter 7 shows that the multitude of people saved during the great tribulation are praising Jesus and have found everlasting peace and security in him (Revelation 7:15–17). We close out the message of the seals with the end of the reign of the RCC with a verse that indicates God has decreed a change in the church:

> When he opened the seventh seal, there was silence in heaven for about half an hour. Then the seven angels who had the seven trumpets prepared to sound them. (Revelation 8:1)

Remember that scroll that provided the future of the church that had two sides? I'll bet that Jesus has just flipped the scroll and is about to read the other side—he is returning to earth to take over his church!

In this one very short verse, the seventh seal reveals the period of the church that occurs after the reign of the RCC ends; we already read verses that tell of the change coming to the church, and now Revelation 8:1 tells us, when combined with Revelation 20:5, that the reign of Jesus will follow the reign of the RCC and it will last for 1,000 years. The first six seals covered the time of AD 30–1330, and this final seal covers the time of AD 1330–2330. We discussed this period thoroughly in *Unraveling Daniel,* but we will go through it again briefly here.

The Transition and Seventh Seal

Why would heaven go silent? There is only one reason for it—Jesus has left the room. Heaven is a noisy place with praises of Jesus and if heaven goes silent, Jesus must not be there anymore. There are two times when Jesus leaves heaven—when he came to earth to replace the sacrifice and when he leaves heaven to reign over the church (Revelation 20:4). The first occasion is the reason for the praising of Jesus, therefore, this silence of "about half an hour" *must* be due to Revelation 20:4—there is no other possibility. Combining Revelation 20:4 and 8:1 we find that the "about half an hour" of heaven time is equal to 1,000 years.

Previously we mentioned that the hour of Jesus will be full of antichrists who want the church for themselves (1 John 2:18-19) and that this hour will be a time when those who reject Jesus and follow false teachers will face trial to be judged (Revelation 3:10). Backing out the numbers of the thousand-year reign of Jesus we know that since his reign started in AD 1330 and will last 1,000 years, it will end in AD 2330—the time decreed for the New Covenant of Jesus (Daniel 8:13–14). With AD 1330 as a key date decreed by God for the ending of the reign of the RCC, what do we find from history that happened in that year? Repeating from before, a man named John Wycliffe, who was born in AD 1330, will translate scripture so that all people will have access to the words of Jesus—the church was freed from the control of the RCC—Jesus will rule over the church.

Four Trumpets of the Reign of Jesus

CHRONOLOGICALLY, FOLLOWING THE VISION John received, with Revelation 8:1 we found ourselves in the reign of Jesus—the thousand–year period that started in AD 1330 and will last until the time of the end in AD 2330. The last part of the first verse of chapter 8 in the book of Revelation mentions the beginning of the message of the trumpet blasts (Then the seven angels who had the seven trumpets prepared to sound them). We will start the analysis of this message of these trumpet blasts by putting them into context; each blast appears to be catastrophic. The seven trumpets announce tragedy, death, and turmoil in the church. As you will soon see, the reign of Jesus is not a period of love, joy, butterflies, and everybody singing kumbaya; it is a period of tragedy and more widespread destruction of the church. Daniel 9:26 prophesies, "War will continue until the end, and desolations have been decreed." Jesus came to take back his church but there will be a continual spiritual battle in it until the end.

The seven trumpets summarize the spiritual battle that began once Jesus returned to reign over the church with his martyrs in AD 1330. The angels are given trumpets to make announcements as an offering is presented at the altar:

DECODING REVELATION

> And I saw the seven angels who stand before God, and seven trumpets were given to them. Another angel, who had a golden censer, came and stood at the altar. (Revelation 8:2–3)

Every angel of God (seven angels who stand before God) will announce the following complete message (seven trumpets) to the complete church. John witnesses another angel bringing "a golden censer" to the altar (came and stood at the altar). Per the Merriam–Webster online dictionary, a *censer* is "a covered incense burner swung on chains in a religious ritual," therefore, John is witnessing a "religious ritual" offering to God. As I read this, I thought back to my days attending an RCC Mass and watching the priest with a consortium of other participants slowly and solemnly walk down the main aisle of the church to the altar while smoke is billowing out of a fabulous-looking incense burner being swung back and forth with each step. It was a fabulous show that had my full attention, but sadly, my focus was on the ritual and not on Jesus.

Apparently, I was not alone feeling like this religious procession did not set my mind on Jesus because Jesus condemns this church ritual:

> He was given much incense to offer, with the prayers of all God's people, on the golden altar in front of the throne. The smoke of the incense, together with the prayers of God's people, went up before God from the angel's hand. Then the angel took the censer, filled it with fire from the altar, and hurled it on the earth; and there came

Four Trumpets of the Reign of Jesus

peals of thunder, rumblings, flashes of lightning and an earthquake. Then the seven angels who had the seven trumpets prepared to sound them. (Revelation 8:3–6)

If you recall, Revelation 5:8 referenced elders with harps singing praises to Jesus who were "holding golden bowls full of incense which *are* the prayers of God's people." In that passage, the prayers of the people *were* incense—they were one and the same. Here they are not—they are two separate entities mixed in the censer. The "smoke of the incense, *together* with the prayers of God's people, went up before God." The prayers are not the sweet offering of incense—they went up *together* with the incense—they are separate. Apparently, the incense is most of the focus of the church rather than the praise and worship of Jesus because "He was given *much* incense to offer."

In Revelation chapter 5, the sweet offering of the prayers that focused on Jesus were presented to God at his throne then the elders of the churches and the worshippers broke out in praise and the prayers were accepted. Here there is a different reaction. You've heard the old Elvis Presley song, "Return to Sender"? This incense smoke offering was not only returned to sender, but it was also violently rejected with a demonstration of how angry Jesus is that they even made it through an elder to his throne. This offering should never had made it to the altar through a church elder, and this angered Jesus because it is coming from false teachers. We get the usual signs from heaven demonstrating the power of God (and there came peals of thunder, rumblings, flashes of lightning), but this time we have destruction presented too (and an earthquake). An earthquake has been added to a previous description of God's words in verse 4:5 of Revelation (From the throne came flashes of lightning, rumblings and peals of thunder) noting that the reaction to this prayer mixture is not a pleasant one—it will cause destruction. You think God is mad and doesn't like the offering? You think God wants his people focusing on the swinging burning censer? If you do, reread that last section of scripture and focus on verse 8:6—the part where the censer is filled with "fire from the altar" and Jesus rejects it "and hurled it on the earth."

John has just witnessed the reason for the coming wrath of God and now John is going to get the details. The worship of Jesus Christ is being corrupted with things other than sincere prayers to Jesus, and Jesus has condemned this practice. Even though Jesus has returned to take the church from the RCC, the church will not be entirely focusing on Jesus as described in chapters 4 and 5 of Revelation and Jesus is angry. Jesus emphatically rejects the ceremonial additions to the prayers of God's people. I hope all of you church leaders with your rules, dress-up costumes, and rigid traditional processions including the burning of incense take note of what has just been presented in this scripture. Jesus is not impressed with these additions to a church service; they make him mad, and he outright rejects and returns them to you with a message to STOP! The apostles didn't describe this form of worship in any of their documentation, therefore, they don't belong in the church. The elders have the guidelines as to how the church is to operate; hear and live the words of Jesus and praise him with all your heart and soul—and that is all!

We now understand the scope of the message of the trumpets; the reign of Jesus will be a time of turmoil consisting of

Four Trumpets of the Reign of Jesus

insincere prayers being mixed up with those who are following and praising Jesus and the trumpets will announce the effects of this damage. Each of the next four trumpet blasts will provide details of a portion of the church that during the reign of Jesus is corrupting the worship of Jesus. Since each of the four trumpet blasts are affecting "a third" of the church, four times a third would be 133% of the church and we can't have that. The most we can have is 100% of the church being affected—the total church. Therefore, we can confidently claim that these trumpet blasts defining specific aspects of corruption in the church will overlap with each other. In summary, the entire church will be affected by these aspects, but some churches will have more than one aspect of a trumpet blast affecting them.

I'm not going to try to determine which organization or branch of church is described by each of these individual trumpet blasts because there isn't any value in it. However, as the old saying goes, "If the shoe fits, wear it," and I recommend that church leaders take note and change worship practices to focus only on Jesus; remove all the extras described in these next four trumpet blasts that aren't necessary and get in the way of focusing on Jesus. The first trumpet blast tells us that during the thousand-year reign of Jesus some of the church will create their own scripture that doesn't even include the worship of Jesus:

> The first angel sounded his trumpet and there came hail and fire mixed with blood, and it was hurled down on the earth. A third of the earth was burned up and a third of the trees were

burned up, and all the green grass was burned up. (Revelation 8:7)

Hail is a sign of condemnation of those who reject God (Revelation 16:21). In addition, the following verse helps us understand the meaning of this trumpet blast:

> The hail will come down on every man and animal that is found in the field, and isn't brought home, and they will die. Those who feared Yahweh's word among the servants of Pharaoh made their servants and their livestock flee into the houses. Whoever didn't respect Yahweh's word left his servants and his livestock in the field. (Exodus 9:19–21)

One-third of the church will completely ignore the words of Jesus to teach a message that is coming from the world (hurled down on the earth). Every church offering this false worship is not from God and will be destroyed (A third of the earth was burned up). The elders of the church that allow this will also be condemned (a third of the trees were burned up) and everyone hearing the message and following it will also be condemned (and all the green grass was burned up).

Then we find that there will be a portion of the church who changes the words of Jesus:

> The second angel sounded his trumpet and something like a huge mountain, all ablaze, was thrown into the sea. A third of the sea turned into blood, a third of the living creatures in the

Four Trumpets of the Reign of Jesus

sea died, and a third of the ships were destroyed. (Revelation 8:8–9)

As we have already stated, the presence of God is associated and represented with mountains. Some of the church will provide a different foundation than what the APC is based on—it is not created on the mountain of Jesus or the mountain of the word of Jesus. The portion of the church being addressed in the second trumpet blast is very large and widespread and it is teaching *something that is like Jesus*, but it is not 100% Jesus as it should be. The teachings of these false teachers are very appealing and leave followers on fire (all ablaze) craving for their words. The sea of the living water of Jesus—the church—is no longer crystal clear (Revelation 4:6), it is tainted with the blood of the rider of the red horse—the dragon (Revelation 6:4). A third of the church will be teaching a Jesus who is not from scripture (A third of the sea turned into blood) and those that follow these words will die (a third of the living creatures in the sea died). The elders providing this tainted message of Jesus will also die (a third of the ships were destroyed).

The third trumpet blast announces that scripture has been widely corrupted through tradition:

> The third angel sounded his trumpet and a great star, blazing like a torch, fell from the sky on a third of the rivers and on the springs of water—the name of the star is Wormwood. A third of the water turned bitter, and many people died from the waters that had become bitter. (Revelation 8:10–11)

Wormwood is another name for tradition—such as the Gospel names provided by the RCC, the story of Patmos and John in prison, etc. We have written extensively about how Jesus and the disciples condemned tradition, but here we read of the damaging effects of tradition that has worked its way into the entire church. Words of tradition will be passed down to the church as though it is from God (a great star, blazing like a torch), and its use will affect a good portion of the words of Jesus (fell from the sky on a third of the rivers and on the springs of water). The mix of tradition with the words of Jesus will result in a message this is sour (a third of the water turned bitter) and although a major portion of the message of Jesus has been tainted with tradition, not all who hear tradition will die. However, much of the church will focus on tradition rather than Jesus and anyone who falls into this trap and puts their faith in tradition rather than Jesus, will die (and many people died from the waters that had become bitter).

For the meaning of *wormwood,* refer to Mark 9:48 that verifies worms in hell. In addition, picture wood that has been rotted so bad that there are worms present in it. If you've ever had to work with rotted wood around your house, you will know what I mean. The surface of rotted wood may appear to be undamaged, but if you take a screwdriver and poke the wood, you quickly puncture the surface and find that just underneath the surface the wood is greatly damaged. Tradition in scripture may sound and appear good, but below the surface, the Word of God is damaged by it.

We have one more trumpet blast describing false teaching in the church:

Four Trumpets of the Reign of Jesus

> The fourth angel sounded his trumpet, and a third of the sun was struck, a third of the moon, and a third of the stars, so that a third of them turned dark. A third of the day was without light, and also a third of the night. (Revelation 8:12)

The sun, moon, and stars have one thing in common—they all provide light. Jesus is the light of the world, and he told his disciples that they are to be the light. A third of the church will cherry-pick scripture and only teach bits and pieces of Jesus that support a message they want to provide, rather than the message that Jesus provided. False teachers will very carefully select what portion of scripture to teach and then they will intentionally ignore the rest because it won't support their corrupt and immoral message (a third of the sun was struck, a third of the moon, and a third of the stars). The full light of Jesus will never be taught in this portion of the church so all who hear and follow this message will be without Jesus (so that a third of them turned dark).

A perfect example of this can be provided by a church I examined that identified themselves as "Presbyterians." I found it odd that there was no mention of the Bible in their values or beliefs page. I searched a bit further and found the following scriptural reference on their "Values and Beliefs" Internet page:

> But the fruit of Spirit is love, joy, patience, kindness, goodness, faithfulness, gentleness, self-control; against such things there is no law. (Galatians 5:22–23)

DECODING REVELATION

The people I know who attend this church are supportive of behavior condemned by scripture, therefore, I investigated further and found the following scripture just prior to the scripture they referenced in the introduction to their church:

> Now the deeds of the flesh are obvious, which are: adultery, sexual immorality, uncleanness, lustfulness, idolatry, sorcery, hatred, strife, jealousies, outbursts of anger, rivalries, divisions, heresies, envy, murders, drunkenness, orgies, and things like these; of which I forewarn you, even as I also forewarned you, that those who practice such things will not inherit God's Kingdom. (Galatians 5:19–21)

Adding the rest of the scripture to the two verses they referenced in Galatians provides a completely opposite message from the one they teach in their assembly. Yes, the part of the scripture they cherry-picked for their beliefs page was important, but so was the rest of the message from the apostle Paul that put behavior into context. This church was cherry-picking their message to ensure that scripture matched their behavior so they wouldn't have to change for Jesus. As a side note, when I brought this aspect of their church up to my acquaintance, he sent me a response listing all the good deeds that this church had done in the name of Jesus. Unfortunately, no amount of work can replace the acceptance of the sacrifice of Jesus for our sin, and the spreading of immoral behavior by their church will only result in death.

Four Trumpets of the Reign of Jesus

Like the first four seals provided an overall summary of the reign of the RCC from AD 30 to 1330, the first four trumpet blasts have provided us an overall summary of the church during the next period of the church that we have referred to as the reign of Jesus that started in AD 1330 and will last until AD 2330. As we mentioned, there are overlaps in the groups that have been discussed, but with those four rejections of Jesus together with those that are saved by the gift of Jesus, the first four trumpet blasts have addressed the total population of the church.

The Time of the End and Three Woes

WE HAVE JUST BEEN presented the details of the reign of Jesus through the first four trumpets and, together with the seven seals, we have a complete description of the church for its 2,300 years of existence—based on Daniel and Revelation calculations of prophecy (Daniel 8:14, Revelation 8:1 and 20:3). What's left but details of the time of the end, and this is what we expect and find as we move forward in Revelation. The time of the end will be a very sad time for those who reject Jesus:

> As I watched, I heard an eagle that was flying in midair call out in a loud voice: "Woe! Woe! Woe to the inhabitants of the earth, because of the trumpet blasts about to be sounded by the other three angels!" (Revelation 8:13)

A *woe* is defined by the Merriam–Webster online dictionary as "a condition of deep suffering from misfortune, affliction, or grief." By the specific wording *"inhabitants of the earth"* we know that these trumpet blasts will provide us details about what will happen to those who decide to follow evil rather than putting their trust and faith in God. We learn from this verse that there will be three woes experienced by the inhabitants of the earth—those who embrace Satan. Eagles are known for their eyesight, therefore, the three woes are certainly related to what Jesus has seen—and you must be assured that he sees everything. Jesus will be pouring out his wrath on the "inhabitants of the earth" in response to what he sees.

The fifth trumpet blast starts out with a recap of Jesus returning to earth to reign:

> The fifth angel sounded his trumpet and I saw a star that had fallen from the sky to the earth. The star was given the key to the shaft of the Abyss. When he opened the Abyss, smoke rose from it like the smoke from a gigantic furnace. The sun and sky were darkened by the smoke from the Abyss. (Revelation 9:1–2)

Twice in Revelation we read about the key to the Abyss—here and in verse 20:3, where Jesus throws Satan into the Abyss, locks him in, and seals it shut for 1,000 years. Luke 8:31 tells us that demons begged Jesus not to send them to the Abyss, therefore, we know that if the demons don't want to go there, it is a horrible place. We also know from both these scripture verses that Jesus has the key to the Abyss. Therefore, with Jesus being the only one with the key to the Abyss, the star that fell from the sky to earth had to be Jesus. Jesus came to earth to reign over the church with his 144,000 martyrs in AD 1330 and his reign will last 1,000 years (Revelation 20:3). The next verse tells us that Jesus releases Satan from the Abyss, therefore, the 1,000 years must be over, and the world is in the time

The Time of the End and Three Woes

of the end (After that he must be set free for a short time) in AD 2330. After Satan is released (When he opened the Abyss, smoke rose from it like the smoke from a gigantic furnace), there is darkness in the world (The sun and sky were darkened by the smoke from the Abyss).

Once Satan is released from the Abyss, he will go on the attack:

> And out of the smoke locusts came down on the earth and were given power like that of scorpions of the earth. They were told not to harm the grass of the earth or any plant or tree, but only those people who did not have the seal of God on their foreheads. They were not allowed to kill them but only to torture them for five months. And the agony they suffered was like that of the sting of a scorpion when it strikes. During those days people will seek death but will not find it; they will long to die, but death will elude them. (Revelation 9:3–6)

At first, the devil will not attack anyone having their name in the book of life (they were told not to harm the grass of the earth or any plant or tree, but only those people who did not have the seal of God on their foreheads). Satan will be allowed to torture but not kill the inhabitants of the earth for five months (They were not allowed to kill them but only to torture them for five months).

Five months seemed like an unusual length of time, so I did some searching and found a reference in the Gospel of Luke to a five-month period. Luke 1:11–17 tells us that God made a promise to Elizabeth and Zechariah that they would have a son—John the Baptist—who would prepare the way for the Messiah. Because Zechariah was old and Elizabeth was on in years (Luke 1:18), Elizabeth went into seclusion for the first five months of pregnancy (Luke 1:25) to protect the birth of John the Baptist. There is only one aspect of the church left and that is the eternal church, so this five–month period must be in preparation for the coming of the eternal church of Jesus Christ. This five-month period will be a time of complete agony for the inhabitants of the earth who will want to die to escape their misery, but God will not allow them to die (During those days people will seek death but will not find it). In addition, just as John the Baptist was protected for five months in preparation of the coming Messiah, those followers who are left on earth are protected for five months to usher in the coming of the eternal church of Jesus Christ.

Next, we learn of the attacks by Satan on the inhabitants of the earth (Revelation 9:7–10). Then we learn that the devil is the leader of the inhabitants of the earth:

> They had as king over them the angel of the Abyss, whose name in Hebrew is Abaddon and in Greek is Apollyon (that is, Destroyer). The first woe is past; two other woes are yet to come. (Revelation 9:11–12)

Satan is the king of the inhabitants of the earth and the wrath of God will be poured out on them because they will choose to follow evil. The first woe is the misery that the wrath of God brings on the inhabitants of the earth after Satan is released from the Abyss to return to the earth and wreak havoc.

The sixth trumpet blast coincides with the sixth bowl of wrath at the time of the end (Revelation 16:12–16) as Satan prepares his army for the final battle between good and evil—the battle of Armageddon:

> The sixth angel sounded his trumpet, and I heard a voice coming from the four horns of the golden altar that is before God. It said to the sixth angel who had the trumpet, "Release the four angels who are bound at the great river Euphrates. And the four angels who had been kept ready for this very hour and day and month and year were released to kill a third of mankind. The number of the mounted troops was twice ten thousand times ten thousand. I heard their numbers. (Revelation 9:13–16)

This "sixth" trumpet blast certainly seems like the sixth bowl of the plague that is poured out on the "great river Euphrates and the water was dried up" to prepare for a battle between the remainder of the church and the forces of evil that prepare for the final worldwide battle. The mounted troops seem like the ones described that are numbered like the sand on the seashore who will attack the few remaining followers of Jesus who reside in a camp (Revelation 20:7–10). The end is coming! There will be a precise set time (this very hour and day and month and year) for the angels who were protecting the world from this great battle (were released to kill a third of mankind). "Twice ten thousand times ten thousand" is 200,000,000 soldiers so there is a great army of "mounted troops" that will assemble for this battle. I added up the total active-duty and reserve soldiers for the top ten countries and they came to less than 30,000,000. Therefore, 200,000,000 troops indicates that what is described here is the final world war that will involve every country and soldier available.

John is seeing this vision of the future in the first century AD, therefore, many of the weapons of war that we are familiar with would be frightening and confusing to him:

> The horses and riders I saw in my vision looked like this: Their breastplates were fiery red, dark blue, and yellow as sulfur. The heads of the horses resembled the heads of lions and out of their mouths came fire, smoke and sulfur. A third of mankind was killed by the three plagues of fire, smoke and sulfur that came out of their mouths. The power of the horses was in their mouths and in their tails; for their tails were like snakes, having heads with which they inflict injury. (Revelation 9:17–19)

These are details of a battle that will happen just over three hundred years from now. Soldiers and robots will be wearing armor (their breastplates were fiery red, dark blue, and yellow as sulfur) and I could guesstimate who the colors refer to, but why try because it is well into the future. John sees moving entities that he calls horses, but they are likely armored battle vehicles and more robots armed with cannons and guns firing through the air with the glow of their firepower appearing like snakes in the air.

Then, John is told that the people of the world will remain stubborn and shake their fists in anger at the Lord—they will not repent and accept the worship of Jesus:

> The rest of mankind who were not killed by these plagues still did not repent of the work of their hands; they did not stop worshiping demons, and idols of gold, silver, bronze, stone and wood—idols that cannot see or hear or walk. Nor did they repent of their murders, their magic arts, their sexual immorality or their thefts. (Revelation 9:20–21)

We were told in the previous verses that a third of mankind were killed in the first phase of the wrath of God being poured out in the form of a fierce battle and at least one of the plagues described in the seven bowls of wrath. Here we read that the "*rest* of mankind who were not killed by these plagues still did not repent of the world of their hands," and this means that *all the remaining* people of the world are corrupt because none of them are repenting. Yes, this is the end because the bowls of plagues have been poured out (The rest of mankind who were not killed by these plagues) but the people did not repent and change their ways—just like Israel of the Old Testament with its cycle of sin, punishment, and repentance. Revelation 22:11 tells us that evil will continue to do evil and those who do good will continue to do good and this is a prime example of it.

DECODING REVELATION

People will not repent from their evil ways—they will refuse to believe that there is a God who will judge and condemn them.

Prior to the announcement of the seventh trumpet that will announce the end, John is provided another piece of the puzzle:

> Then I saw another mighty angel coming down from heaven. He was robed in a cloud, with a rainbow above his head; his face was like the sun, and his legs were like fiery pillars. (Revelation 10:1)

John witnesses another angel coming down from heaven with a message from Jesus (his face was like the sun). The message will be one that addresses the foundation of the church (and his legs were like fiery pillars). The message continues:

> He was holding a little scroll, which lay open in his hand. He planted his right foot on the sea and his left foot on the land, and he gave a loud shout like the roar of a lion. When he shouted, the voices of the seven thunders spoke. And when the seven thunders spoke, I was about to write, but I heard a voice from heaven say, "Seal up what the seven thunders have said and do not write it down." (Revelation 10:2–4)

We know that the big scroll written on both sides and sealed with the seven seals was all about Jesus and his church. Now John is told there is another scroll—a little one and the angel that holds this scroll does not require Jesus to read it, it is being delivered by an angel with one foot planted in the Word of

The Time of the End and Three Woes

God present in the church (the sea) and one foot planted on the earth with the people of the world (left foot on the land). This message is about a bridge between heaven and earth. It is a very powerful and complete message (Seal up what the seven thunders have said), but Jesus does not want this part of the message to be told (and do not write it down). Thunder is the first indication of a violent storm that is moving in, and Jesus provides John the full details of the coming storm (seven thunders), but this part of the message will remain sealed, and you will understand why Jesus wanted it sealed when we go through the rest of the vision.

Jesus' sacrifice was for the Jews, but we know from Old Testament prophecy that the promise of the Messiah was to be extended to all people (Genesis 22:18, Psalm 22:27 and 86:9, and Isaiah 9:2, 42:1, 49:6, among many others). The bridge spoken about in Revelation 10:2–4 will be a big event that will formally extend the promised gift of the Messiah to the Gentiles, and the little scroll has all the details.

But first, John receives the details of how the final trumpet blast will end the church on earth:

> Then the angel I had seen standing on the sea and on the land raised his right hand to heaven. And he swore by him who lives for ever and ever, who created the heavens and all that is in them, the earth and all that is in it, and the sea and all that is in it, and said, "There will be no more delay! But in the days when the seventh angel is about to sound his trumpet the mystery of God

will be accomplished, just as he announced to his servants the prophets." (Revelation 10:5–7)

The angel proclaims, "There will be no more delay!"—the end is coming and that means judgment is on the way. The sixth trumpet described a five-month period of the wrath of God poured out on the inhabitants of the earth, then afterward will come the battle of Armageddon, and finally, the end will come with the sounding of the seventh trumpet. In the days when the final trumpet sounds the angel proclaims that the "mystery of God will be accomplished." However, before Jesus tells John about the seventh trumpet, Jesus has a message for John that needs to be told that will help explain the meaning of the seventh trumpet. The time of the end means that there will be judgment and with the completion of judgment all prophecy proclaimed to the prophets of old will be complete and finished—the mystery of God will no longer be a mystery—it will be done! I realize we haven't completed the explanation of the "three woes" entirely, but that message will continue to be cleared up in the following chapter.

15

Two Witnesses Welcome the Gentiles

WITH THE FIFTH AND sixth trumpets, John's vision entered the time of the end in AD 2330. The first woe described the inhabitants of the earth experiencing the wrath of God for their rejection of Jesus to follow evil. After the sixth trumpet there is a sidebar for Jesus to show John how the last two woes tie into this period of the time of the end. Previous scripture introduced the little scroll as a bridge to heaven, then John starts to get the details of this bridge:

> Then the voice I had heard from heaven spoke to me once more: "Go, take the scroll that lies open in the hand of the angel who is standing on the sea and on the land." So I went to the angel and asked him to give me the little scroll. He said to me, "Take it and eat it. It will turn your stomach sour, but in your mouth it will be as sweet as honey. I took the little scroll from the angel's hand and ate it. It tasted as sweet as honey in my mouth, but when I had eaten it, my stomach turned sour. (Revelation 10:8–10)

DECODING REVELATION

Jesus tells John (the voice I had heard from heaven) that the next message that John will receive is one that like the story of Jesus and the transition periods of the church described in the big scroll, has been decreed by God (the scroll that lies open in the hand of the angel). The message of the little scroll describes the bridge that will bring the Word of God (standing on the sea) to the rest of the world—the Gentiles (and on the land).

Jesus warns John to carefully digest this next message (Take it and eat it) because what is revealed will make him sick (turn your stomach sour), but not to worry because the message is a good one (but in your mouth it will be as sweet as honey). Why is this message going to make John sick? Because God decreed that there will be a sacrifice of blood to welcome the Gentiles to join God's people for the salvation of Jesus, and John will recognize the two witnesses of the sacrifice as the apostles Peter and Paul. John is being told of the horrible death of his two friends that will make him sick, but he will also see how their sacrifice was intended to formally offer the blood sacrifice of Jesus for the forgiveness of sins to the Gentiles. Flash back to our analysis of 2 Peter and remember how John, Peter, and Paul were together in the final days of the two witnesses writing their farewell letter to the church. All three of these disciples will play a major role in extending the sacrifice of Jesus to the Gentiles, so it will be a sweet message that will make them sick because it is a physical death sentence for them. We now know why Jesus wanted the message of the seven thunders remain sealed.

The sacrifice of the two witnesses will formally extend the sacrifice of Jesus to the Gentiles. If you're puzzled about why this is necessary, please read the following:

Two Witnesses Welcome the Gentiles

> Jesus went out from there and withdrew into the region of Tyre and Sidon. Behold, a Canaanite woman came out from those borders and cried, saying, "Have mercy on me, Lord, you son of David! My daughter is severely possessed by a demon!" But he answered her not a word. His disciples came and begged him, saying, "Send her away; for she cries after us." But he answered, "I wasn't sent to anyone but the lost sheep of the house of Israel." (Matthew 15:21–24)

The Jewish prophets prophesied the Messiah would come for God's people and then Jesus came and fulfilled prophecy. Jesus' sacrifice was in fulfillment of a promise to the Jews. However, we know from the rest of this story that Jesus had compassion on this woman and extended his gift to her because of her faith:

> But she came and worshiped him, saying, "Lord help me." But he answered, "It is not appropriate to take the children's bread and throw it to the dogs." But she said, "Yes, Lord, but even the dogs eat the crumbs which fall from their master's table." Then Jesus answered her, "Women, great is your faith! Be it done to you even as you desire." And her daughter was healed from that hour. (Matthew 15:25–28)

Jesus extended his grace to a Gentile woman on this one occasion as an exception. What is described in the little scroll is a sacrifice that will formally welcome *all* the Gentiles into the covenant of God through faith in Jesus. Afterward, no longer will there be Jews and Gentiles—all people will be treated the same; everyone will have access to the gift of Jesus.

Peter and Paul were commissioned by Jesus as missionaries to the Gentiles. Jesus told Peter that he would be sacrificed:

> "Most certainly I tell you, when you were young you dressed yourself and walked where you wanted to. But when you are old, you will stretch out your hands, and another will dress you and carry you where you don't want to go." Now he said this, signifying by what kind of death he would glorify God. (John 21:18–19)

The Holy Spirit used Peter as the initial instrument to accept the Gentiles into the family of God and for the apostles to consider them equal to the Jews (Acts 10:9–11:18). Peter informed the Gentiles of their acceptance into the kingdom of God (Acts 10:44), then the Holy Spirit entered the Gentiles.

The apostle Paul was also commissioned by Jesus to be a sacrifice for the Gentiles:

> I said, 'Who are you Lord?' "He said, 'I am Jesus, whom you are persecuting. But arise, and stand on your feet, for I have appeared to you for this purpose: to appoint you a servant and a witness both of the things which you have seen, and of the things which I will reveal to you; delivering you from the people, and from the Gentiles, to whom I send you, to open their eyes, that they may turn from darkness to light and from the power of Satan to God, that they may receive

Two Witnesses Welcome the Gentiles

> remission of sins and an inheritance among those who are sanctified by faith in me.' (Acts 26:15–18)

There can be no debate about Paul's mission to the Gentiles and his persecution for sharing the word of Jesus with them (Romans 11:13, Galatians 2:2, and many more). In Acts 26:18, we see how Jesus informed Paul that he would be sacrificed for the Gentiles (that they may receive remission of sins).

The next verse of Revelation ensures that we know the two witnesses are the sacrifice for the Gentiles:

> Then I was told, "You must prophesy again about many peoples, nations, languages, and kings." (Revelation 10:11)

The little scroll is a prophecy about "*many* peoples, nations, languages, and kings." John has just been told that the message in the vision he is about to receive will apply to "many" people of the world—and not just the Jews. The two witnesses will invite *all* people of the world to share in the sacrifice of Jesus and although not *all* will accept the sacrifice of Jesus, *many* will accept and be saved. Jesus was the big scroll, but the little scroll will be men who will provide an offering for the Gentiles.

The message of the little scroll starts with John receiving details of the rejection of the Gentiles:

> I was given a reed like a measuring rod and was told, "Go and measure the temple of God and the altar, with its worshippers. But exclude the outer court; do not measure it, because it has

> been given to the Gentiles. They will trample on the holy city for 42 months. (Revelation 11:1–2)

John was asked to measure the church with its worshippers, but not to include the area outside the temple allocated to the Gentiles—they have not yet been formally accepted into the church of Jesus Christ. The Holy City is mentioned four times in Revelation with this being the first. The other three mentions of the Holy City are all in Revelation chapter 21 and reference the eternal church. This story is about the entry into the eternal church—the invite! This invitation to the Gentiles is not about extending the boundaries of the church to an unholy people—it is about welcoming the Gentiles into the Holy City—the eternal kingdom. But, sadly, Jesus says that the Gentiles will join with the Jews to trample on Jesus. Why is forty-two months important? Jesus, during his mission, was trampled on for 42 months by the Jews and the Gentiles will trample on the two witnesses and their message about Jesus for the same length of time.

The next verses provide details of this mission of the two witnesses:

> And I will appoint my two witnesses, and they will prophesy for 1,260 days, clothed in sackcloth. They are "the two olive trees" and the two lampstands, and "they stand before the Lord of the earth." (Revelation 11:3–4)

In these verses, Jesus provides the direct connection of the two witnesses to his own mission (And I will appoint my two witnesses)—they were decreed for 1,260 days—just like the mission of Jesus was decreed at 1,260 days (Revelation 12:6).

Two Witnesses Welcome the Gentiles

Since 1,260 days can also be a representation of forty-two months, we know that, like "a time, times, and half a time" references a decreed period of time, so does forty-two months.

We search for prophecy in scripture to help us understand the description of the *"the two olive trees"* and we find it in the Old Testament:

> And I further answered and said to him, "What are these two olive branches that drip into the receptacles of the two cold pipes from which the golden oil drains?" then he answered me and said, "Do you not know what these are?" And I said, "No, my lord." So he said, "These are the two anointed ones, who stand beside the Lord of the whole earth." (Zechariah 4:12–14)

Most of us have heard the old saying about "extending an olive branch" to end a disagreement or confrontation. The Jews and Gentiles have been divided since God chose the people of Israel to call them his own. The Jews and Gentiles remained enemies throughout Jesus' ministry, but the Lord is showing John that the decreed time for change will soon arrive. Zechariah prophesied that the two witnesses will be an invitation (olive branches) to settle these differences between the Jews and the Gentiles. They will be the vessel of God (gold pipes) that will extend to them the gift of Jesus Christ (from which the golden oil drains). Two witnesses have been chosen (There are two anointed ones) as substitutes of Jesus (who stand beside the Lord) to extend the sacrifice of Jesus to all sinners (of the whole earth).

Returning to Revelation 11:3–4, we find that these two witnesses will be blessed and holy (dressed in sackcloth) and will provide the message of Jesus Christ, the light of the world (lampstands) that will spread through the whole world, to the Gentiles (stand before the Lord of the earth). From www.bibletools.org/index.cfm/fuseaction/Topical.show/RTD/CGG/ID/5902/Clothed-with-Sackcloth.htm, we obtain a great summary of what it means to be *"clothed in sackcloth."* We learn that the Bible has several meanings behind *being clothed in sackcloth*; "mourning, repentance, humble, austerity, and poverty." The characteristics of the two witnesses are like those of Jesus.

They will also have miraculous powers like Jesus:

> If anyone tries to harm them, fire comes from their mouths and devours their enemies. This is how anyone who wants to harm them must die. They have power to shut out the heavens so that it will not rain during the time they are prophesying; and they have the power to turn the waters into blood and to strike the earth with every kind of plague as often as they want. (Revelation 11:5–6)

They will burn and kill anyone who tries to harm them with flames that come out of their mouths, they will stop the rain from falling, turn water into blood, and they will cause plagues to strike as often as they want. Does this sound like they are to be *like* Jesus? The little scroll should make more sense to you now. Jesus is the big scroll, these two witnesses are the little

Two Witnesses Welcome the Gentiles

scroll—they are like Jesus, but nobody can be Jesus; they pale in comparison, but they have a similar mission to complete! I hope that by now you are also thinking about the fire that burned down Rome in AD 64 with the ongoing debate about how it started. Revelation tells us how the fire started! Peter and Paul burned down the city of Rome (fire comes from their mouths and devours their enemies) then were transported to Jerusalem to be executed.

The miraculous story about the works, persecution, and then the deaths of the two witnesses continues in the following prophecy:

> Now when they have finished their testimony, the beast that comes up from the Abyss will attack them, and overpower and kill them. Their bodies will lie in the public square of the great city—which is figuratively called Sodom and Egypt—where also their Lord was crucified. (Revelation 11:7–8)

Jesus was executed outside the city gates of the city of Jerusalem, and we are told that these two witnesses will be martyred at the same location (where also their Lord was crucified). They will be persecuted by those who worship evil (the beast that comes up from the Abyss) then they will be executed for their faith, brought back to life after three and a half days, then ascend into heaven just as their Lord did.

At this point, I'm going to return to the very key word in verse 11:7, the *"beast."* We have already referred to the beast as the RCC numerous times, based on our investigation into

Daniel captured in *Unraveling Daniel* and what we will present later in this book. Here we get confirmation that the beast is a demon that has come up "from the Abyss" to attack, overpower, and kill them. We have confirmation in this verse that the beast—the RCC *is in fact* the synagogue of Satan that was described by Jesus in Revelation chapters 2 and 3 and was present in the church from the beginning.

The follow-up verses 11:9 through 11:12 provide the details that the substitute sacrifice of Peter and Paul on behalf of Jesus will be rejected by the Gentiles:

> For three and a half days some from every people, tribe, language and nation will gaze on their bodies and refuse them burial. The inhabitants of the earth will gloat over them and will celebrate by sending each other gifts, because these two prophets had tormented those who live on the earth. (Revelation 11:9–10)

Jesus wants John to know that the missions of the two witnesses and Jesus are not exactly the same. The two witness will be dead but not buried for "three and a half days" versus the three days Jesus spent in the grave. However, like the Jews who rejected the sacrifice of Jesus, the Gentiles (The inhabitants of the earth) will not only reject their sacrifice they will celebrate the executions of Peter and Paul. Recall that "the inhabitants of the earth" are the ones who will experience an "hour of trial" that is coming (Revelation 3:10), who will be judged to avenge the blood of the martyrs (Revelation 6:10), and will experience the 'three woes' (Revelation 8:13). The inhabitants of the earth will be those who join the beast to persecute and kill those in the church of Jesus Christ.

The story of the two witnesses ends with the following scripture:

> But after three and a half days the breath of life from God entered them, and they stood on their feet, and terror struck those who saw them. Then they heard a loud voice from heaven saying to them, "Come up here." And they went up to heaven in a cloud, while their enemies looked on. At that very hour there was a severe earthquake and a tenth of the city collapsed. Seven thousand people were killed in the earthquake, and the survivors were terrified and gave glory to the God of heaven. (Revelation 11:11–13)

The two witnesses are again like Jesus, but they are not Jesus. They were executed like Jesus, then spent three and a half days dead and unburied versus the three days Jesus spent in the grave. They ascended to heaven like Jesus did, but we don't hear that they made appearances for forty days. Did they make appearances for forty days like Jesus? We can't say for sure because all the documentation of the two witnesses has been removed and deleted or stored in a hidden vault somewhere in the Vatican. How can I make this claim? There are only two men in history who fulfill this prophecy, and these are the apostles Peter and Paul. Of course, you could ignore Peter and Paul and claim that the two witnesses are some mysterious people yet to come in some seven-year great tribulation period fable made-up from prophecy in Daniel. We already proved those stories about Daniel 9:27 pointing to the future seven-year tribulation and the Antichrist to be a myth. In addition, we've already proven that according to Revelation chapter 7, the great tribulation happened during the time of the beast. If this vision is about two witnesses in the distant future, then what was it in this message that made John sick to his stomach while the message tasted sweet? Is it just about general suffering as the theological stew claims, or is it very personal to John? I think we can say without a doubt that it was very personal to John and this proves that Peter and Paul are the two witnesses and that John is with them in the end.

Jesus even told Peter that John would survive this event and Peter wouldn't:

> Then Peter, turning around, saw a disciple following. This was the disciple whom Jesus loved, the one who had also leaned on Jesus' breast at the supper and asked, "Lord, who is going to betray you?" Peter seeing him, said to Jesus, "Lord, what about this man?" Jesus said to him, "If I desire that he stay until I come, what is that to you? You follow me." This saying therefore went out among the brothers, that this disciple wouldn't die. Yet Jesus didn't say to him that he wouldn't die, but, "If I desire that he stay until I come, what is that to you?" This is the disciple who testifies about these things, and wrote these things. We know that his witness is true. There are also many other things which Jesus did, which if they

would all be written, I suppose that even the world itself wouldn't have room for the books that would be written. (John 21:20–25)

Based on this there were rumors about John remaining alive until the end, but this was not what Jesus meant. John was decreed by God to survive the executions of Peter and Paul to deliver the last letter from these three now called 2 Peter. John lives on through the Revelation he received and documented prior to the execution of Peter and Paul in AD 64/65, and the delivery of their last letter, 2 Peter.

If you're still saying, "But wait, we don't have any records of Peter and Paul breathing fire, stopping the rain for forty-two months, or turning water into blood," we don't have recorded documentation of a lot of things. And, we know that those in charge of the church *could not* have Peter and Paul as the two witnesses because it would destroy the RCC's reign over the church through Peter. We were required to read between the lines to find out who wrote the letter 2 Peter to determine what happened to Peter, Paul, and John and we found the breadcrumbs of clues to piece history together.

The only historical characters that fulfill the description of the two witnesses would be the disciples Peter and Paul. Think about two men who are spreading the Word of God like wildfire and who we know through existing documentation, have been persecuted. We know that the apostle Paul has been persecuted many times and nearly killed, then his words go silent (Acts 28:30–31). When I read those two verses in Acts, I think that there was more written that described the deaths of Peter and Paul as the two witnesses. But naysayers could state, "But wait, John, this doesn't match the estimated date of Paul's death from the NIV AD 67/68." There is a lot of disputing about when Paul died, and various sources provide dates from AD 62 to 68. We also know from history that Peter is persecuted and likely killed, based on the documentation from the First Epistle of Clement to the Corinthians.

From scripture we know that there is a great earthquake just like there was at the exact times Jesus was crucified (Matthew 27:54) and when Jesus rose from the dead (Matthew 28:2). I couldn't find a recorded earthquake that struck Jerusalem when the two witnesses were executed, but then again, I couldn't find evidence of a recorded earthquake at the time Jesus died either. Does this mean that these things didn't happen because they aren't verified by other historical records? You need to note that I said *"other historical records"* because the Bible is a historical record proven time and time again to be true. It's easy to look at the prophecy and state that this summary is all wrong because there is no second set of historical records that verify these things, including these earthquakes in Jerusalem. We do know that earthquakes are common in Jerusalem and in Rome, therefore, these earthquakes are very likely. We have very limited documentation of the many things that happened in the days of the apostles as they started the church, but we can assemble the pieces and prove that they occurred!

Another possibility is that the earthquakes could be symbolic. For example, since *"seven"* means complete and Revelation 11:13 tells us "Seven thousand people were killed in the earthquake," we can interpret the earthquake as signifying complete devastation of the Gentiles who reject the sacrifice, and that all those who don't receive a sentence of death will find the Lord

Two Witnesses Welcome the Gentiles

and be saved (and the survivors were terrified and gave glory to the God of heaven).

We promised to deal only in facts, so here are the facts about the apostles Peter and Paul that prove they were commissioned by Jesus to be the substitute sacrifice for the Gentiles:

1. The message was sweet to John but made him sick because he was being shown the beautiful mission of his friends and the horrible death that they would experience that he would be present for.
2. Peter and Paul had missions just like Jesus:
   a. length of the mission of the two witnesses was protected for exactly the same number of days as the length of Jesus' mission—1,260 days as specified in Revelation 12:6,
   b. they both healed people (Acts and the letters of Paul),
   c. they both preached and taught the Word of God (Acts and the letters of Paul),
   d. they were the only apostles recorded to have brought people back from the dead like Jesus did (Acts 9:36–43 and 20:7–12),
   e. their ministry was protected until their decreed death just like the ministry of Jesus' mission was,
   f. they were prophesied to be executed, remained dead for an extended period of time to prove that they were dead, then came back to life, and,
   g. they ascended into heaven.
3. The two witnesses breathed fire down from heaven to destroy their enemies which matches the time frame of the mysterious fire that burned down Rome about the

time these two would have been executed—AD 64—and coincided with historical facts about these two men going silent; and finally,

4. The letter 2 Peter as we previously determined, places Peter, Paul, and John together penning a farewell letter to the church.

Peter and Paul were the sacrifices and it made John sick because he would be present for and witness what was prophesied.

We have one final two-part question to address as we wrap up the story of the two witnesses described in chapter 11 of Revelation: "Why was the message of the two witnesses presented near the end of the trumpet blasts?" and "What happened to the other two woes?" The rest of chapter 11 will clear this up:

> The second woe has passed; the third woe is coming soon. (Revelation 11:14)

The first woe was the pain and agony of the inhabitants of the earth at the time of the end as they follow the devil into battle against the good of God. This second woe was caused by the "inhabitants of the earth" rejecting their formal invitation into the kingdom of God through the sacrifice of the two witnesses, therefore, they will face judgment. The two witnesses formalized the invitation of all people and languages to the wedding supper of the Lamb (Revelation 19:9) but the inhabitants of the earth declined that invitation, and now they will face judgment—the third woe (Revelation 3:10).

The third woe is not specifically mentioned in Revelation, but we can be certain we know what it is—it is the seventh

Two Witnesses Welcome the Gentiles

trumpet that will condemn the inhabitants of the earth that have been judged. We were told that the trumpets would usher in the three woes and now we are at the last trumpet blast ushering in the third woe:

> The seventh angel sounded his trumpet, and there were loud voices in heaven, which said, "The kingdom of the world has become the kingdom of our Lord and of his Messiah, and he will reign for ever and ever." (Revelation 11:15)

The last trumpet blast (the seventh angel sounded his trumpet) starts with a message from the throne of Jesus (and there were loud voices in heaven). God, who had set up his kingdom on earth through Jesus (which said, "The kingdom of the world has become the kingdom of our Lord and his Messiah."), will now have the final kingdom in heaven where it will exist forever ("and he will reign for ever and ever"). The Reign of Jesus has ended, and the wrath of God has been poured out on the inhabitants of the earth for rejecting God's son. The "inhabitants of the earth" have been judged and there is one final act from God—condemnation of them to a permanent death with Hades closely following (Revelation 1:18, 6:8, 20:13, and 20:14).

Heaven is rejoicing that Jesus has returned and he is now setting up his final kingdom with his eternal church called the new Jerusalem:

> And the twenty-four elders, who were seated on their thrones before God, fell on their faces and worshiped God, saying: "We give thanks to you, Lord God Almighty, the One who is and who

> was, because you have taken your great power
> and have begun to reign. (Revelation 11:16–17)

The elders praise God for allowing them to preach the Word that resulted in many entering the kingdom of heaven. The elders fall face down in praise of Jesus because he has returned to heaven to reign over his eternal kingdom. But not everyone is happy:

> The nations were angry, and your wrath has come. The time has come for judging the dead, and for rewarding your servants the prophets and your people who revere your name, both great and small—and for destroying those who destroy the earth. (Revelation 11:18)

We learned earlier at the end of the sixth trumpet blast that the people of the earth did not repent and welcome Jesus into their life. The time has come for sentencing those who rejected Jesus, and what could be more terrible than an eternal death sentence in misery (and for destroying those who destroy the earth)? On the flip side, those that followed Jesus are not dead and they will now receive their reward (rewarding your servants and prophets and your people who revere your name).

The last portion of this vision is John seeing Jesus as the ark of the covenant in the temple in heaven:

> Then God's temple in heaven was opened, and with his temple was seen the ark of his covenant. And there came flashes of lightning, rumblings,

peals of thunder, an earthquake and a severe hailstorm. (Revelation 11:19)

The judgment will come from the throne of God and then Jesus is pictured as the ark of the covenant. God will destroy the earth (an earthquake and a severe hailstorm) at judgment time.

The first half of Revelation has taken John and us, the future readers of Revelation, through the entire future of the church. You will now see how the second half of the book of Revelation, chapters 12 through 22, will do the same starting from the beginning of the church.

The Woman and the "Seven" of Jesus

THE FIRST HALF OF the book of Revelation presented a complete presentation of the church from start to finish. Chapters 1 through 5 put the book into context and provided the disciples with the status of the current church and the organization chart and operations manual for how the church is to function. Chapters 6 through 11 of Revelation took us on a brief chronological journey of the church starting with the arrival of Jesus and ending with judgment and the arrival of the eternal church. As we start chapter 12, we expect to read another chronological presentation of the church with more details and after receiving a long and heavy dose of heartburn and frustration, that is what we found. I say *"heartburn and frustration"* because I am a perfectionist who needs to completely believe in the final product and decoding prophecy required numerous iterations of baby-step interim conclusions to complete the puzzle. As the Lord kept revealing details to me like peeling away the layers of an onion, my eyes continued to see more and more of the truth.

As we presented in the previous book *Unraveling Daniel*, chapter 12 of Revelation is crucial to understanding and unraveling the seventy sevens presented in Daniel 9:24–27. Many theologians and preachers tell us that the *"seven"* mentioned in the book of Daniel's seventy "sevens" prophecy is about a future coming Antichrist. For example, from the NIV we obtain the following explanation:

> 9:27 *He will confirm a covenant . . . will put an end to sacrifice.* According to some, a reference to the Messiah's ("the anointed one," v.26) instituting the new covenant and putting "an end" to sacrificial system; according to others, a reference to the antichrist's ("the [ultimate] ruler who will come," v.26) making a treaty with the Jews in the future and then disrupting their system of worship. *Abomination that causes desolation.* See note on 11:31.
>
> Note on 11:31—the altar to the pagan god Zeus Olympius, set up in 168 BC by Antiochus Epiphanes and prefiguring a similar abomination that Jesus predicted would be erected in the future (see MT 24:15; Luke 21:20 and notes).
>
> Note on MT 24:15 . . . .

There are two possibilities—the *seven* is either a reference to Jesus or theologians have created a map to get readers to a mysterious seven-year tribulation and Antichrist period at the time of the end. The future Antichrist theory conveniently steers the church away from identifying and confronting the beast. Approaching prophecy in pieces while selecting certain strategic passages and a story of the distant future can be created, but this is not the intent of this prophecy. The "seventy sevens"

The Woman and the "Seven" of Jesus

of Daniel is about Jesus and nothing else, and with a message of Jesus, the whole landscape changes because the mysterious seven years of Jesus must be resolved from Revelation.

We coined the term *commonly accepted theological stew* or CATS in *Unraveling Daniel* to describe some of the stories created by theologians that do not have a factual basis, but can be assembled from scripture to point readers away from the beast. John in a Patmos prison was one of these made-up stories that pointed readers from the truth about the two witnesses that if the truth were known would destroy the RCC's reliance on Peter overseeing the church. Similarly, in chapter 12, if the woman of Revelation becomes the church, then the beast is exposed as the RCC and Daniel and Revelation can be assembled to tell the complete truth of prophecy—and it is not an overall good one for the church.

Consider that per www.biblegateway.com the term *"beast"* is mentioned in the NIV thirty-six times and that thirty-four of the references to it are in the book of Revelation. The beast, as discussed in the New Testament, is addressed almost entirely in Revelation yet the church ignores the beast. I've been told that the message the Lord wants me to provide is that the beast in the church is to be exposed and addressed. Corruption in the church was prophesied to run rampant, but when is the last time you have heard a preacher or teacher of the word tell you that in a church service? I can't recall a preacher or teacher ever addressing the beast besides generic, useless comments pointing to the future. The Lord has made it clear that the church moving forward is to change. The choice is in the hands of the elders as I wrote a pastor of mine several weeks ago—the church will have two options—continue to hide the beast in the future, or deal with a beast that is visible and present in the church in fulfillment of prophecy. The beast has been in the church since the beginning, it has not left the church, and it will not leave the church. Evil will remain prominent in the church because many stand to lose wealth, prestige, and power if it is removed.

Continuing with our verse-by-verse analysis, if the *seventy sevens* is all about the coming of Jesus, the *seven sevens* becomes Jesus with a seven-year mission to create Jesus' church. Using this concept from Daniel, we can determine the meaning of the woman presented in Revelation to start chapter 12:

> A great sign appeared in heaven; a woman clothed with the sun, with the moon under her feet and a crown of twelve stars on her head. She was pregnant and cried out in pain as she was about to give birth. (Revelation 12:1–2)

First, let me present the NIV Study Bible interpretation of the *woman:*

> 12:1—*a woman clothed with the sun.* Perhaps a symbolic reference to the believing Messianic community (see v. 5), though some believe "woman" refers specifically to Israel (see note on v. 7; for the imagery, cf. Ge 37:9–10).

Initially, I wasn't completely sure I was understanding the scripture—was there more than one woman? The woman will keep changing and this indicated more than one woman, but Revelation 12:1 is the first mention of fourteen references to

The Woman and the "Seven" of Jesus

"the woman," therefore, it seemed as though there was only one.

As I prayed over this for several weeks, I received a few visions from the Holy Spirit:

> May 3, 2022—I was looking for our boat cover and John had taken it somewhere for some reason. We went to the sporting goods store to retrieve it and there was a mast of a large sailboat in the way so we moved it, but even after moving it I couldn't find the boat cover. I called John over for help and he was nonsensical and I wondered if he was drunk.

> May 6, 2022—The part of the book of Revelation I will look at this morning is related to what I have already examined. The subject today will be tied to previous work.

The first vision troubled me, because I have a son named John and, at first, I wondered if I was receiving a message about him and his family. I wrote a message to my daughter-in-law and asked her if everything was alright, and I received an affirmative that it was. As a funny sidenote, our daughter-in-law has been great keeping us in the loop with our two grandkids because they live over two thousand miles away and we don't get to see them that often. After my text asking her how they were doing, I received special attention in the way of videos and pictures. I am blessed!

The first vision seemed to tell me that I was looking for something but those trying to explain it to me were nonsensical and seemingly drunk. Hmm . . . I recalled the woman being connected with others getting drunk off her wine, so I searched Revelation for this term and found the following references to the woman being drunk:

> I saw that the woman was drunk with the blood of God's holy people, the blood of those who bore testimony to Jesus, When I saw her, I was greatly astonished. (Revelation 17:6)

> For all the nations have drunk the maddening wine of her adulteries. The kings of the earth committed adultery with her, and the merchants of the earth grew rich from her excessive luxuries. (Revelation 18:3)

Wow! I thought—that is revealing. I finally realized that in Revelation 12:1–2 there can be only one entity called a *"woman"* that "appears in heaven," is "clothed with the sun, with the moon under her feet" (Jesus) and "a crown of twelve stars on her head" (the disciples)—the church. Remembering from my February 2022 visions that the book of Revelation is all about the church was crucial in helping me to understand this concept. The church starts out as Jesus who is holy with the disciples who help start the church, then ends up as the "Mother of all Prostitutes" in Revelation 17:3–6. The woman morphs over time from something that is pure to something that is completely evil. My early May 2022 visions indicated that I was looking for something that was hidden and covered up—in a theological stew, but a drunk person would be the key and the message is the same as what it was before—all about the church.

The Woman and the "Seven" of Jesus

As I pondered the meaning of "the woman with twelve stars and the child" in this chapter, I looked up to see the most beautiful sunrise I have ever seen; it was an incredible experience. The sunrises in Melbourne Beach, Florida, over the ocean, are usually fabulous, but this morning it was as though the full eminence of God was shining on me in vivid colors through clouds strategically positioned to make me say "WOW!" God had just provided me the answer to my prayers about understanding the book of Revelation, and the beauty of the light shone on me as I praised God for giving me this insight this morning. I wanted to break away and type this because I was worried about forgetting the message, but I couldn't look away from the beauty of the colors that shone over the strategic clouds in rays that seemingly spread over the universe.

Jesus confirmed this meaning of the woman in words that John documented:

> A woman, when she gives birth, has sorrow because her time has come. But when she has delivered the child, she doesn't remember the anguish any more, for the joy that a human being is born in the world. Therefore you now have sorrow, but I will see you again, and your heart will rejoice, and no one will take your joy away from you. (John 16:21–22)

What is the disciple's job when Jesus leaves? Jesus commissioned them to start and grow the church (Matthew 28:18–20). After they receive the Holy Spirit, they will start Jesus' church—and that includes documenting his words that will last forever

(Luke 21:32–33). The church started out pure then became corrupted and was even completely taken over by the RCC; therefore, if the woman and her characteristics is an entity called "the church," she will change over time, and everything makes sense. Try to separate them like the boat cover, the mast, and the boat itself in my vision, and it becomes nonsensical.

Revelation already provided the summary of the church starting out pure then becoming corrupted: Jesus rode out on a white horse to conquer sin (first seal—Revelation 6:2), then the devil got involved in the church (second seal—Revelation 6:4), and the church together with false teachers morphed into something that forced people to work for salvation (third seal—Revelation 6:5–6). The church became the RCC that would force the world to join their corrupt church under the threat of persecution, death, and isolation from society (fourth seal—Revelation 6:7–8). The RCC caused grave damage and killed a set number of those dedicated to the words of Jesus Christ (fifth seal—Revelation 6:9–11) and removed any traces of the church that the apostles started (sixth seal—Revelation 6:12–7:17). Finally, Jesus returned to remove the stranglehold the RCC had over the church and free the words of Jesus to be taught throughout the world (seventh seal—Revelation 8:1). Even after Jesus returned to reign over the church in AD 1330, the church was not to be pure again—the words of Jesus were now accessible to all, but the church remains in disarray until the time of the end (Revelation chapters 8, 9, and 11) with the coming of the eternal church.

Back to Revelation 12:1–2, God decreed that the church was with God and was God, then God decreed that Jesus would be born (She was pregnant and cried out in pain as she was about

The Woman and the "Seven" of Jesus

to give birth) to start the church on earth. Right up front, Jesus tells John that the devil tried to prevent the birth of the church of Jesus:

> Then another sign appeared in heaven: An enormous red dragon with seven heads and ten horns and seven crowns on its heads. Its tail swept a third of the stars out of the sky and flung them to the earth. The dragon stood in front of the woman who was about to give birth, so that it might devour her child the moment he was born. (Revelation 12:3–5)

The church has an overwhelming uphill battle to get its footing because even when Jesus is born, Satan and the religious leaders are out to destroy him. The religious leaders (seven heads) and the law they profess to follow (ten horns) together with the politicians in charge (seven crowns on its heads), went on the attack to remove Jesus from the earth as soon as he was born (The dragon stood in front of the woman who was about to give birth, so that it might devour her child the moment he was born). We see how King Herod tried to kill Jesus after he was born (Matthew 2), and if he had been successful, Jesus never would have lived to sacrifice his life for sin and the church would never have started.

Before we move on, I believe there is another message buried in the details of these verses that bears mentioning. There is an interesting concept in Revelation 12:1 that I want you to consider. There are twelve stars mentioned and this certainly represents the twelve disciples but remember, one of the disciples was corrupt and his corruption brought about his death prior to the starting of the church. We learn from scripture that Matthias was chosen by the disciples to replace Judas who betrayed Jesus (Acts 1:12–26), but we read in scripture that Jesus chose someone else who was crucial to the start-up and spread of the church—the apostle Paul. We never hear of Matthias again outside of the disciple's selection of him as a replacement, yet Jesus reached out to Paul and told him he had a mission. Jesus said of Paul in Acts 9:15, "For he is my chosen vessel to bear my name before the nations and kings, and the children of Israel." It's obvious that Paul is the Lord's chosen replacement for Judas, and Paul fought for this recognition. I suggest you read the first chapter of Galatians to see how Paul knew Jesus through "revelation from Jesus Christ."

The next verses verify how God protected Jesus during his ministry to start the church:

> She gave birth to a son, a male child, who "will rule all the nations with an iron scepter. And her child was snatched up to God and to his throne. The woman fled into the wilderness to a place prepared for her by God, where she might be taken care of for 1,260 days. (Revelation 12:5–6)

The woman starts out as Jesus being born and when he is born, although he is in human form, he is with God in Spirit (And her child was snatched up to God and to his throne). Jesus starts his mission and needs the protection of God, so God decreed 1,260 days for the mission of Jesus—the first half of the seven of Jesus specified in Daniel 9:27. If God had

The Woman and the "Seven" of Jesus

not protected the mission of Jesus (The women fled into the wilderness for a place prepared for her by God), Satan would have killed Jesus and the church would never have been started (where she might be taken care of for 1,260 days)—see John 12:23, 35 and 13:19 as a few of the many references to God's protection until the decreed time of the sacrifice arrived. We noted earlier how the 1,260 days represented the mission of Jesus written on the big scroll for the Jews, and the mission of the two witnesses written on the little scroll for the Gentiles. Verses 12:5–6 present the first half of the mission of Jesus specified in Daniel 9:24–27—his ministry with the disciples by his side for 1,260 days of preaching, teaching, and healing.

The following passages tell us that evil was hurled to the earth and that God protected the church from destruction:

> Then war broke out in heaven. Michael and his angels fought against the dragon, and the dragon and his angels fought back. But he was not strong enough, and they lost their place in heaven. The great dragon was hurled down—that ancient serpent called the devil, or Satan, who leads the whole world astray. He was hurled to the earth, and his angels with him. (Revelation 12:7–9)

This is in the past for John as he reads this summary. After Jesus sacrificed himself for the sin of the world, Satan started a spiritual war. Jesus succeeded in fulfilling his mission, and now that Jesus has returned to heaven after his ascension the devil made his presence known and started a battle for the church. We know from Revelation chapters 2 and 3 that the synagogue

of Satan was already in the start-up church (The great dragon was hurled down—that ancient serpent called the devil, or Satan). With that fact together with Revelation 12:7–9 we can be assured that Satan entered the church immediately after the sacrifice of Jesus was completed.

Jesus commissioned the disciples to start the church, but Satan did not want to allow it:

> Then I heard a loud voice in heaven say: "Now have come the salvation and the power and the kingdom of our God, and the authority of his Messiah. For the accuser of our brothers and sisters, who accuses them before our God day and night, has been hurled down. (Revelation 12:10)

The good news is that people have a path to salvation (Now have come the salvation and the power and the kingdom of our God) through Jesus and *his* church (and the authority of his Messiah). The bad news is that a great evil presence is attacking the church when God's people are just getting started (For the accuser of our brothers and sisters, who accuses them before our God day and night has been hurled down).

The next verse is very telling because we learn of the disciple's full dedication to fulfill the mission Jesus gave them—to start the church:

> They triumphed over him by the blood of the Lamb and by the word of their testimony; they did not love their lives so much as to shrink from death. (Revelation 12:11)

The Woman and the "Seven" of Jesus

God decreed that the disciples *will* win the battle against Satan (They triumphed over him) through their acceptance of the sacrifice of Jesus (by the blood of the Lamb). As commissioned by God (Matthew 28:18–20) they have already started documenting their testimony of Jesus as the foundation for the church (and by the word of their testimony). The disciples believed in Jesus so much that they sacrificed their lives to fulfill their commitment to Jesus to start the church (they did not love their lives so much as to shrink from death). Revelation 12:11 tells us that *all* the disciples were martyred for their dedication to starting and growing the church for Jesus.

The disciples are blessed but those who oppose the disciples, Jesus, and the church they are starting, are cursed:

> Therefore rejoice, you heavens and you who dwell in them! But woe to the earth and the sea, because the devil has gone down to you! He is filled with fury, because he knows that his time is short. (Revelation 12:12)

The people who pay attention to the message of the disciples will be happy because they have been saved through the blood of Jesus just as the disciples have been (Therefore rejoice, you heavens and you who dwell in them!). But remember the three woes for the inhabitants of the earth? Those who oppose Jesus, the inhabitants of the earth, will have a painful existence and death. The followers of Jesus will have peace for eternity, but the inhabitants of the earth will have nothing but pain (But woe to the earth) because they have corrupted the words of Jesus in the church (and the sea). The devil will stop at nothing to

destroy the church using the people who follow Satan (He is filled with fury, because he knows that his time is short).

Jesus and the disciples were protected for 1,260 days to complete the mission of Jesus, but the work is not complete yet and the devil is still in pursuit to destroy the church before it is even started:

> When the dragon saw that he had been hurled to the earth, he pursued the woman who had given birth to the male child. (Revelation 12:13)

Satan is hot on the trail of the disciples to prevent them from completing the start-up of the church. But just as God decreed a protected period for the mission of Jesus, he also decreed a protected period for the disciples to do the groundwork to provide a solid foundation for the church, such as documenting the words of Jesus and spreading the Word to start churches in various locations:

> The woman was given the two wings of a great eagle, so that she might fly to the place prepared for her in the wilderness, where she would be taken care of for a time, times, and half a time out of the serpent's reach. (Revelation 12:14)

First, we learned how God decreed and protected the birth of Jesus, then we learned in Revelation 12:6 that the mission of Jesus with his disciples was decreed and protected for 1,260 days. Here in Revelation 12:14 we learn that the disciples are protected for a decreed period of *"a time, times, and half a time."* Most theologians believe that *"a time, times, and half a time"* refers to "three and a half years" based on *"a time"* being equal to a year. The exact number of days the apostles were protected is specified in Daniel 12:11–12, and when calculated it is about three and one-half years (please see *Unraveling Daniel* for a complete analysis, explanation, and the exact number of days). In *Unraveling Daniel* we also found that if *"a time"* is ten years *"a time, times, and half a time"* can also refer to the execution of the two witnesses that came thirty-five years after the sacrifice of Jesus, and if *"a time"* is one hundred years *"a time, times, and half a time"* will refer to the decreed time of the signing of a formal agreement between the RCC and the Roman Government to persecute followers of Jesus who reject their religion (*The Edict of Thessalonica* signed in AD 380 which is 350 years after the sacrifice of Jesus). The decreed length of time for *"a time, times, and half a time"* seems to change with the length of time allocated to *"a time."*

If God would not have intervened, the powerful religious leaders in combination with the political powers would have destroyed the church from the beginning. Just for your own information, there are two other references to a *"time, times, and half a time"* in scripture and they are both in Daniel. The "holy people will be delivered" into the hands of the beast (Daniel 7:25) for 1,300 years, and the time that "the power of the holy people has been finally broken" is set so that all things will be completed (Daniel 12:7); both are set times—"a time, times, and half a time." These, like the period allocated to start-up the church, are set decreed times by God and cannot be changed or altered.

DECODING REVELATION

The devil who is intent on destroying the church with the help of the false teachers and the government who will join them, attack Jesus and the start-up church:

> Then from his mouth the serpent spewed water like a river, to overtake the woman and sweep her away with the torrent. But the earth helped the woman by opening its mouth and swallowing the river that the dragon had spewed out of his mouth. (Revelation 12:15–16)

If you wondered about the details of the takeover of the church, you don't need to wonder any more. As soon as the set time of protection is over, the evil entity we know as the beast from Daniel, spews words from the devil that it says are from God (from his mouth the serpent spewed water like a river) and their words and actions are used to attack the church and control it (to overtake the woman and sweep her away with the torrent). The inhabitants of the earth—those who follow evil (But the earth)—support Satan and the evil false teachers (helped the woman by opening its mouth) to overtake the church with appealing words that replace the words of Jesus (and swallowing the river that the dragon had spewed out of its mouth). *Torrent* is another word for "fast-flowing water" and the false teachers speak in articulate and enticing words that are quickly and forcefully substituted for the words of Jesus. We learn that the woman is no longer pure (But the earth helped the woman by opening its mouth) because it has embraced and accepted the words of Satan (and swallowing the river that the dragon had spewed out of his mouth).

The Woman and the "Seven" of Jesus

The takeover of the church by the synagogue of Satan is quick and total:

> Then the dragon was enraged at the woman and went off to wage war against the rest of her offspring—those who keep God's commands and hold fast their testimony about Jesus. (Revelation 12:17)

Part of the church remains loyal to the words of Jesus (Then the dragon was enraged at the woman), so Satan and the false teachers attack those who remain loyal to the disciples and the words of Jesus (and went off to wage war against the rest of her offspring). Most have joined the false church but those who do not succumb to the words of Satan provided by the false teachers (those who keep God's commands and hold fast their testimony about Jesus) are attacked.

This story certainly reads as a very quick transformation of the church from the greatness and good of Jesus to complete corruption. The woman as the church transformed from the purity of Jesus to the evil entity called the "RCC," then continued to morph over time. We have the evidence from the apostle's writing about their persecution by the false teachers and how disappointed and full of grief they were about those trying to stop the spread of the church or change it to something other than what Jesus wanted (1 John 2:18–19 is a prime example). It doesn't get any better for the woman as time goes on as you will read in the next several chapters. Even when Jesus returned to reign over the church in AD 1330 the church remains corrupt. However, at that time at least the Word is free from the reign of the great false church and people will be able to choose whether to follow the words of Jesus or the words of mere men.

In summary, Revelation is prophecy that accurately predicted the start of the church and how it was immediately corrupted. With this knowledge, my advice to you as we move forward is to realize and accept that the woman with the crown of twelve stars giving birth was Jesus, the disciples, and the Church all wrapped up into one, and she will change from the essence of purity and goodness to become something very undesirable.

The Reign of the RCC

Another chronological summary of the future of the church began with the birth of the church in chapter 12 of Revelation. The key words in that last verse of chapter 12 were that there will be a war waged *"against the rest of her offspring,"* referring to a great spiritual battle between those that follow the disciple's documentation of the words of Jesus and the synagogue of Satan decreed to take over the church. It's open season for Satan and his followers to persecute and even execute those refusing to follow their words rather than the words of Jesus. As chapter 12 was ending, John's vision revealed how effective the RCC was at both persuading (Revelation 12:16) and forcing people to join their ranks (Revelation 12:17).

As we start chapter 13, we find details of the union between the RCC and Satan:

> The dragon stood on the shore of the sea. And I saw a beast coming out of the sea. It had ten horns and seven heads, with ten crowns on its horns and each had a blasphemous name. (Revelation 13:1)

John sees Satan (The dragon stood) at the foot of the church of Jesus Christ (on the shore of the sea) and observes a beast coming out of the church (I saw a beast coming out of the sea). The origin of the beast will be from within the church—it will be a homegrown coup of false teachers that are embedded in the church—the "synagogue of Satan." *Seven horns* represent the complete power of God (Revelation 5:6), but this evil entity does not have the power of God, it created its own temporary power by enforcing their law. The synagogue of Satan morphs into the RCC that will throw away the Ten Commandments and mandate their law for the church (ten horns). The RCC, like the beast described in Daniel, will have complete control over everything in the church (seven heads) and those desiring to find Jesus will be required to follow *their* law. The RCC will claim to be God and say that they are speaking for Jesus, but they are not (and each had a blasphemous name).

John is provided more details about the beast that came out of the church:

> The beast I saw resembled a leopard, but had feet like those of a bear and a mouth like that of a lion. The dragon gave the beast his power and his throne and great authority. One of the heads of the beast seemed to have a fatal wound, but the fatal wound had been healed. The whole world was filled with wonder and followed the beast. (Revelation 13:2–3)

The RCC moved fast (The beast I saw resembled a leopard) stomping out anything in its way (but had feet like those of a bear) while using bold, forceful, fierce, and commanding speech they claim is from Jesus (and a mouth like a lion). We are told again that the devil (The dragon) gives the RCC (gave the beast) its power and authority (his power and his throne and great authority).

You're about to receive a "WOW" moment as we continue our analysis here. God tells John how the RCC will orchestrate their takeover of the Church—it will be through resurrecting Peter. Peter was executed for his faith as one of the two witnesses, but the RCC brought him back to life (but the fatal wound had been healed) through their popes who they claim are direct descendants of Peter. I struggled with these verses for a long time pondering what they meant before the Holy Spirit opened my eyes to the true meaning. When you consider that the RCC is founded solely on Peter passing on the leadership of the church to successive popes, you understand that the RCC is based entirely on a Peter that never died. You can look for all the details of the RCC takeover of the church through Peter in our previous book *The Early Church Father Catholic Fraud*, but the RCC's Catholic Catechism manual, "English translation of the Catechism of the Catholic Church for the United States of America copyright © 1994," provides all the evidence you need. The *"Church"* throughout the *Catechism of the Catholic Church* is a reference to *only* the Catholic Church who claims that Jesus chose Peter to lead the apostles and start their church, the one and only church, and that through them and only them, the church exists and continues. Peter is resurrected and remains alive in the Catholic Church (Peter *will remain* the unshakable rock of the Church) through the succession of popes who fulfill the role of Peter.

You should now be able to recognize the importance of John being an old man in a Patmos prison. If John received this revelation early in church years, the prophecy of the two witnesses *is about Peter and Paul,* and if Peter and Paul *are the two witnesses,* Peter is an *equal* to Paul and no longer "holds the first place in the college of the Twelve" as specified in the RCC *Catechism.* The RCC was built upon a Peter assigned by Jesus to oversee the church and the RCC changed or eliminated anything that contradicted this because it threatened their existence and reign over the church. The false teachers who founded the RCC built a story of Peter as the leader of the disciples and the church and created a theological stew to support their story. John as an old man in Patmos when he received this Revelation steers readers to the future to look for a great Antichrist, rather than proving that Peter was one of the two witnesses who gave his life for Jesus, and that the beast is exposed as the RCC.

Returning to Revelation 13:3 and wrapping up that passage, we find that the RCC battles any dissenters and is victorious in all their battles so the world marvels at their power (The whole world was filled with wonder). The RCC firms up their grip on the church and helps them convert others to join them (and followed the beast). The next verse reveals just how powerful the RCC was prophesied to become:

> People worshiped the dragon because he had given authority to the beast, and they also worshiped the beast and asked, "Who is like the beast? Who can wage war against it?" (Revelation 13:4)

The Reign of the RCC

People in the RCC will ultimately be worshiping the devil (People worshiped the dragon) through their worship and obedience to the beast because the beast is working for Satan (because he has given authority to the beast). People will worship the RCC (and they also worshiped the beast) claiming that that the RCC must be from God because it is so powerful and has total control over the church (and asked, "Who is like the beast?" Who can wage war against it?"). In the past I've heard comments from Catholics that claim *their church must be from God* because it is so large and powerful.

Next, John receives more confirmation that the beast is pretending to be God:

> The beast was given a mouth to utter proud words and blasphemies and to exercise its authority for forty-two months. It opened its mouth to blaspheme God, and to slander his name and his dwelling place and those who live in heaven. It was given power to wage war against God's holy people and to conquer them. And it was given authority over every tribe, people, language and nation. (Revelation 13:5–7)

I believe this to be a reference to the mission of the two witnesses because there are two keys in these verses that point directly to them. *Forty-two months* is mentioned twice in Revelation; we have just read the second and the first was in Revelation 11:2 when John was told that the Gentiles will "trample on the holy city for 42 months." The forty-two months in Revelation 11:2 coincides with the 1,260-day mission of the two witnesses, therefore, the synagogue of Satan (RCC and beast) is persecuting the representatives of Jesus during their imprisonment and mission. The second reason I believe this to be addressing the two witnesses is that the execution of Peter and Paul formally accepted the Gentiles into the family of God. Once the beast kills the two witnesses and that sacrifice is complete, the Gentiles are welcomed into the family of God and the RCC who now already controls the church will have authority over all people (It was given authority over every tribe, people, language and nation). Note that the RCC was "given" the authority by God—he decreed the start and the end of their reign and confirmed it with the prophecy written in Daniel and Revelation.

The transformation of the church to the RCC will, of course, have a very negative effect:

> All inhabitants of the earth will worship the beast—all whose names have not been written in the Lamb's book of life, the Lamb who was slain from the creation of the world (Revelation 13:8)

All who worship the beast rather than Jesus will be considered "inhabitants of the earth" and their names "have not be written in the book of life." This is a very damning assessment of the RCC; if you worship the RCC rather than Jesus, you are condemned. The RCC transformed the church to focus on Peter and tradition and this was not in accordance with the guidance of Jesus and the words of the apostles.

The Reign of the RCC

As I was trying to decode this last section of Revelation, I wondered what was happening to all those people who sincerely were trying to follow Jesus but were being duped by the false teachings of the RCC and other churches. I was distraught at the thought of only 144,000 finding Jesus over 1,300 years of the reign of the RCC, and the RCC still remains a formidable part of the church. I wondered about my father who was a lifetime member of the RCC, but lived as though he was following Jesus. He passed away in 1986 as a member of the great false church, so I wondered if he was saved? This troubled me and I prayed about it for many days asking the Lord to help me understand.

The Holy Spirit provided me a vision with the answer, and it is a good one that helped me understand the multitude saved during the great tribulation (Revelation 7:9):

> August 30, 2022—We were out for a ride on our golf cart then came back to our condo to check on the remodeling work that was ongoing. I found our handyman Julio still hard at work and now my father was helping him. Why is my dad here? There can only be one reason for it—he is alive.

Jesus has condemned the RCC and its followers but, in my vision, Jesus is showing me that my dad is alive. Devout followers of Jesus in the RCC must be saved, because my father who died in 1986 is still alive. Those who follow the RCC and put their faith in them rather than Jesus will be condemned. My father had his faith in Jesus, so he was saved and lives. My father's reliance on Jesus for his salvation resulted in him being

rewarded with eternal life. Yes, he was a member of the RCC who was told by the church leaders to work for his salvation, but he didn't worship the beast—he worshiped Jesus. I never heard my father speak as though the RCC pope was to be worshiped, and he didn't rely on his RCC ticket to get him into heaven regardless of his behavior. I periodically found my father on his knees praying to Jesus and repenting of his sins. Based on the message in this vision from the Holy Spirit, those who rely on the RCC religion to save them will perish, but those who follow and rely on Jesus to save them, will live. If you are a member of the RCC be wise; *do not focus on Peter, tradition, or the things of the RCC, focus all your attention on Jesus!*

Next, the Lord tries to comfort those who will be persecuted for believing in the "simply Jesus" process:

> Whoever has ears, let them hear. "If anyone is to go into captivity, into captivity they will go. If anyone is to be killed with the sword, with the sword they will be killed." This calls for patient endurance and faithfulness on the part of God's people. (Revelation 13:9–10)

Jesus cautions people to listen closely to the words of scripture and understand that Jesus provides a *gift* of salvation (Whoever has ears, let them hear). The RCC will change the message and the words, and they will persecute those who do not agree with them. Reject the RCC demands, and you may "go into captivity" or be "killed with the sword," but Jesus cautions believers to be patient and stick to the truth of only Jesus

The Reign of the RCC

(patient endurance and faithfulness), because if you do, you will be with God (God's people).

The RCC will create the role of a leader to firm up their control over the church:

> Then I saw a second beast, coming out of the earth. It had two horns like a lamb, but it spoke like a dragon. It exercised all the authority of the first beast on its behalf, and made the earth and all inhabitants worship the first beast, whose fatal blow had been healed. (Revelation 13:11–12)

The *"two horns like a lamb"* is a direct reference to the ram with two horns in Daniel 8:3, where we identified it as both covenants of God with his people. This beast says it is Jesus of the New Covenant and represents the law of the Old Covenant (It had two horns like a lamb), but it is not, its words are from Satan (but it spoke like a dragon). The second beast derives its power from the first beast (It exercised all the authority of the first beast on its behalf), therefore, we know it is a representative of the RCC. The pope will require (and made) that everyone on earth (the earth and all inhabitants) revere the RCC (worship the first beast). We again get an affirmation that the RCC is created from the resurrected disciple Peter (whose fatal blow has been healed).

The concept of the *"miracle"* becomes an important aspect supporting the reign of the RCC over the church:

> And it performed many great signs, even causing fire to come down from heaven to the earth in full view of the people. Because of the signs it

was given power to perform on behalf of the first beast, it deceived the inhabitants of the earth. It ordered them to set up an image in honor of the beast who was wounded by the sword yet lived. (Revelations 13:13–14)

If you have some time to kill, I recommend you research the interesting topic of the importance of miracles in the RCC. I won't go into details, but it is a fascinating, expensive, and seemingly profitable business aspect of the RCC that is in accordance with Revelation 13:13–14. Those performing miracles are recognized as saints in the RCC and there are many popes designated as saints. The RCC claims that many, if not most, of their Popes have performed miracles, therefore, this previous passage should not be a surprise (And it performed many great signs, even causing fire to come down from heaven to earth in full view of the people). The signs that God allowed the popes to perform on behalf of the RCC (Because of the signs it was given power to perform on behalf of the first beast) will deceive many people (it deceived the inhabitants of the earth). Worshippers of the pope and the RCC will be required to possess statues and other trinkets that represent the power and might of the RCC (It ordered them to set up an image in honor of the beast who was wounded by the sword yet lived).

The followers of the RCC are relying on statues, idols, and pictures to remind them of Peter, the popes, and famous RCC members and they even put faith in their protective properties. This practice was condemned throughout the Old Testament and throughout the teachings of Jesus, but the beast has promoted idols to be used throughout the church and home. One

The Reign of the RCC

website, www.totallycatholic.com, provided the following description that many should see as idol sale and worship:

> Hugest selection of value-priced Catholic Saints statues on the internet, including: color resin, outdoor, plastic/resin, pocket statues and more! Get a Catholic statue for your home altar, bedroom, kid's room, family room or outdoor garden area. Make the tremendously strong intercessional power of the Communion of Saints a visible part of your home!

> By the year AD 100, Christians were honoring other Christians who had died, and asking for their intercession. Many people think that honoring saints was something the Church set up later, but it was part of Christianity from the very beginning. As a matter of fact, this practice came from a long-standing tradition in the Jewish faith of honoring prophets and holy people with shrines.

Another site I visited called www.catholic.org provided a picture of an important political figure kissing the toe of a statue representing Peter the disciple of Jesus with the following caption:

> After 800 years of kisses (including a peck from Queen Sofia of Spain, pictured in the photo), the big toe of this statue of St. Peter has been rubbed down to a stump. Catholic tradition celebrates

Peter as the first Bishop of Rome and the father of the papacy.

Imagine Jesus' reaction to people kissing the statue of one of his disciples!

Think about the beads of the rosary and the crosses draped around the necks of leaders, teachers, and followers of the RCC. When I graduated from college and was leaving home to travel 2,300 miles away from Michigan to California, my parents gave me a graduation present that was a thin gold chain with a medal of St. Christopher on it to protect me during my travels. They sincerely thought that this idol would help keep me safe. I wore it for years and periodically even wondered about the protection it provided. Some years after I had consistently worn the medal, I heard that the RCC had removed St. Christopher from sainthood. I didn't know if it was true or not, but I thought it interesting and started referring to my necklace as my "Mr. Christopher protective medal."

The power of the pope and the RCC will be so extensive that people will need to be associated with them to participate in commerce:

> The second beast was given power to give breath to the image of the first beast, so that the image could speak and cause all who refused to worship the image to be killed. It also forced all people, great and small, rich and poor, free and slave, to receive a mark on their right hands or on their foreheads, so that they could not buy or sell unless they had the mark, which is the name

The Reign of the RCC

of the beast or the number of its name. This calls for wisdom. Let the person who has insight calculate the number of the beast, for it is the number of a man. That number is 666. (Revelation 13:15–18)

The leader of the RCC (the second beast) promoted the image of the RCC to the point that it appears to have a life of its own (give breath to the image of the first beast) so that the image is so recognized and revered (so that the image could speak) that those who did not pay homage to the image (all those who refused to worship the image) faced death (to be killed). The RCC required (it also forced) everyone (all people) to be recognized (mark on their right hands or on their foreheads) as a member of their false church to participate in commerce (so that they could not buy or sell).

As we mentioned earlier, the RCC does not need you to have a mark on your forehead or wrist to verify that you are following them—they will be able to tell from your actions and words. The RCC will scrutinize the actions of people to ensure they are following the ways of the RCC. The followers of the RCC will be carrying around trinkets like rosary beads or wearing crosses around their necks to ensure the religious leaders know that they are "good Catholics." RCC followers will make the sign of the cross at the appropriate times and attend services mandated and conducted by the RCC. In addition, there is an interesting, ancient, centuries-old RCC ritual of marking the wrists and/or foreheads of the members with ashes to usher in the beginning of the Lenten season that commemorates the death and resurrection of Jesus. Could this ritual also be the fulfillment of the prophecy?

We can't leave these verses without a discussion of the famous number *"666"* presented in Revelation 13:18. *Seven* is the perfect and complete number, therefore, my initial consideration was that *"666"* must be the most incomplete number in scripture. However, we know from that verse that the "person with insight" will be able to "calculate the number of the beast, for it is the number of a man," so it seemed like there was more to this number. After pondering the meaning of this verse for a few days, I prayed for insight one night as I went to bed and woke up the next morning with the following vision:

> March 1, 2023—We had a piece of property that we were going to put our home on. People had control over the foundation, and we were surprised to find that they were filling it up with old, contaminated waste junk, most of which was about 5 feet high. The junk looked like furnace burners with exhaust stacks at the top. The foundation area was packed full of this debris that they were trying to get rid of and cover up. I didn't like this waste put under our future home, but I had no control over the foundation and home construction so there was nothing I could do about it. We were going to have to live with it.

Hmm, I thought . . . people breath in and exhaust waste like one of these pieces of junk that were going to be under the foundation of the house I was building, therefore, could this be signifying that in my vision I was building a house over dead people—over a graveyard? After I pondered the meaning, I went to the computer to search for the origin of a six-foot grave and opened the first site, <u>Why Are Graves Dug 6 Feet Deep? (verywellhealth.com)</u>, which had some very interesting information. Apparently the six-foot grave originated from a London plague that began in 1665 and lasted through 1666. At that time, the authorities issued a guidance called "Burial of the Dead" that required graves to be dug six feet deep to keep animals from digging up corpses and spreading the disease.

Does this have anything to do with the "666" from Revelation 13:18? They both address dead people due to the spread of disease—the one in Revelation is spiritual and the one in history is physical. I wrapped up my thoughts knowing that graves are about six feet wide, by six feet deep, by six feet long (at least in previous centuries). Therefore, the calculation of a death grave for a man is 6 x 6 x 6 and death is represented by the number "666" signifying that those following the beast will face eternal death in Hades following close behind as specified in the fourth seal (Revelation 6:8).

18

The End of the Reign of the RCC

*I*N CONTRAST TO THE number of the beast that we found at the end of chapter 13 of Revelation, we start chapter 14 with John witnessing those sealed with the mark of God:

> Then I looked, and there before me was the Lamb, standing on Mount Zion, and with him 144,000 who had his name and his Father's name written on their foreheads. (Revelation 14:1)

This verse has me confirming that the marks of both God and the devil are on the hearts of people rather than being written someplace on the body. Are these 144,000 walking around with Jesus' name written on their foreheads? Of course not! Just like those walking around marked by the beast, these 144,000 were sealed with the words of Jesus on their hearts. Remember during the opening of the fifth seal when John saw a few souls of martyrs who had been slain for their faith and the souls asked when their deaths would be avenged by the judgment of their executioners? They were told that they would have to "wait a little longer, until the full number of their fellow servants" were killed just as they were (Revelation 6:9–11) and that there would be 144,000 souls martyred (Revelation 7:4–8). We are here! John looks and sees the 144,000 that have been sealed (before me was the Lamb standing on Mount Zion and with him 144,000 who had his name).

John no longer sees *some* souls of martyrs underneath the altar, he sees the 144,000 standing before Jesus on Mount Zion who are sealed by God. It is time for the change from the reign of the RCC to the reign of Jesus. Why Mount Zion? Because Mount Zion represents the presence of God and John is witnessing Jesus with his church. Jesus will be leaving heaven to reign over the earth; the reign of the RCC is ending because the set number of martyrs has been reached. Chronologically, the RCC took control over the church then assigned a leader of their church called the "pope" who substituted for Peter, and persecuted anyone who didn't join their organization. Now, in AD 1330, they have executed 144,000 followers of Jesus who remained loyal to the teaching of the disciples, and this is the decreed end of their rule over the church.

The souls of the 144,000 martyrs who were executed for remaining faithful to Jesus during the reign of the RCC, are excited:

> And I heard a sound from heaven like the roar of rushing waters and like a loud peal of thunder. The sound I heard was like that of harpists playing their harps. And they sang a new song before the throne and before the four living creatures and the elders. No one could learn the song except the 144,000 who had been redeemed from the earth. These are those who did not defile

themselves with women, for they remained virgins. They follow the Lamb wherever he goes. They were purchased from among mankind and offered as firstfruits to God and the Lamb. No lie was found in their mouths, they are blameless. (Revelation 14:2–5)

Just before heaven goes silent (Revelation 8:1) and Jesus returns to the church to rule, the 144,000 were making loud praise noises in heaven that sounded "like that of harpists playing their harps." In addition, they were singing a "new song before the throne" that nobody could learn "except the 144,000 who had been redeemed from the earth." The 144,000 were followers of Jesus who did not succumb to the false teaching of the church under the reign of the beast (These are those who did not defile themselves with women). But why the plural *"women"* rather than the *"woman"* who was noted earlier in Revelation as the church? The church started out as the one true church of Jesus Christ then became corrupted by the RCC —a woman. By the time AD 1330 arrives, the RCC fragmented and split due to tensions in leadership. For example, there was the historical "Great Schism" of 1054 that split the RCC into two separate churches. The 144,000 had no part of these "women" and they were executed for staying true to Jesus (No lie was found in their mouths). They were considered sacrifices to Jesus (They were purchased from mankind and offered as firstfruits to God and the Lamb).

The next verses inform us that the gospel is now free:

> Then I saw another angel flying in midair and he had the eternal gospel to proclaim to those who live on the earth—to every nation, tribe, language and people. (Revelation 14:6)

Jesus has freed the gospel from the grip of the RCC! The words of Jesus that save people from death (the eternal gospel) will no longer be controlled by the RCC; they will now be spread to all people as initially intended when they were documented by the disciples (to proclaim to those who live on the earth). Everyone in the world (every nation, tribe, language and people) will now have access to the words of Jesus. Recall that in AD 1330 John Wycliffe was born who would later translate the Bible into the language of the people so that all can read scripture for themselves; the RCC would no longer be able to control the Word of God. No longer would followers of Jesus be forced to work for salvation; rather than learning about and accepting the gift of salvation from Jesus, they would have a choice. As noted in the third seal, people were starving for the words of Jesus, but the seventh seal that corresponded to the freedom of the Word and the end of the reign of the RCC, has brought Jesus back to earth to reign with his "firstfruits."

The next verse provides a summary of the New Covenant:

> He said in a loud voice, "Fear God and give him glory, because the hour of his judgment has come. Worship him who made the heavens, the earth, the sea and the springs of water." (Revelation 14:7)

The End of the Reign of the RCC

Those who live in the time of Jesus—the New Covenant—are in the hour of judgment, so "Fear God and give him glory"—worship Jesus who created everything (who made the heavens, the earth) and gave you his words for a gift of salvation that you learn about from the church (the sea) that is spreading the words of Jesus (and the springs of water).

We get confirmation that the RCC has lost control over the church:

> A second angel followed and said, "Fallen! Fallen is Babylon the Great, which made all the nations drink the maddening wine of her adulteries." (Revelation 14:8)

Babylon, a great pagan city in the days of Daniel, is mentioned nineteen times in his prophetic book. It's reasonable to assume that when Jesus returns to reign over the church he considers the RCC to be a great pagan empire, referred to now as *"Babylon the Great."* Babylon the Great represents the growth of the RCC into a church that is an enormous pagan kingdom like the Babylon of Daniel's era—it worships idols and has substituted their words for the Word of God. The second angel has just announced that the authority of the RCC has been removed and they are no longer in total control of the church (Fallen! Fallen is Babylon the Great).

Note that Babylon the Great didn't offer their church and worship services to the nations, they *"made all the nations drink"* their maddening wine. In addition, they weren't localized, it was the only game in town for *"all the nations"* and that meant that no matter where you lived, if you wanted to try to follow Jesus, *all* the words about Jesus were filtered through them and were corrupted. Babylon the Great packaged their deception into an appealing and enticing package (the maddening wine of her adulteries) then spread it throughout the nations.

Another angel provides a follow-up message regarding the beast:

> A third angel followed them and said in a loud voice: "If anyone worships the beast and its image and receives its mark on their forehead or on their hand, they too, will drink the wine of God's fury, which has been poured full strength into the cup of his wrath. They will be tormented with burning sulfur in the presence of the holy angels and of the Lamb. (Revelation 14:9–10)

In the future, follow the pagan ways of Babylon the Great to worship the pope and the RCC rather than Jesus, and you will be punished with the wrath of God "poured full strength." This third angel cautions the world as it moves forward that although the beast will not be reigning anymore, it will still spread its enticing message that is like maddening wine. Therefore, heed the warning and do not follow the beast or you too will face the wrath of God. This is a preview of the following chapters. Jesus will show John how those who choose to follow the beast are punished; he warns future generations that following the beast will result in a tortuous eternity. The torment of those following the beast is even specific (tormented with burning sulfur) and the worst part is, they will be able to see what they are missing in heaven (in the presence of the holy angels and of the Lamb).

Follow the beast and you will be punished for eternity:

> And the smoke from their torment will rise for ever and ever. There will be no rest day or night for those who worship the beast and its image, or for anyone who receives the mark of its name. This calls for patient endurance on the part of the people of God who keep his command and remain faithful to Jesus. (Revelation 14:11–12)

Those following the RCC will be punished (smoke from their torment will rise for ever and ever). Jesus reminds the followers of Jesus that the transition from the reign of the RCC to the reign of Jesus will not be an immediate change, therefore, those who seek Jesus will need to be patient (This calls for patient endurance on the part of the people of God) during this transition to remain steadfast in their worship of Jesus (who keep his command and remain faithful to Jesus). Wycliffe is born in AD 1330, but it will be fifty years or so until he translates the Bible, and then it will take many more years before the words of Jesus spread, so Jesus tells those who want to follow him to have "patient endurance" while they remain under the effects of Satan and the beast.

Jesus provides some guidance while the change is taking place:

> Then I heard a voice from heaven say, "Write this: Blessed are the dead who die in the Lord from now on." "Yes," says the Spirit, "they will

rest from their labor, for their deeds will follow them." (Revelation 14:13–14)

Now that the reign of the RCC has ended, people will be able to find the truth in Jesus and we are told that those who are successful will be blessed. During the reign of the RCC people had to work for salvation, but while Jesus reigns they will no longer need to work for it (they will rest from their labor) because their belief in Jesus will result in deeds that prove their dedication to Jesus (their deeds will follow them).

Then we read about how Jesus will harvest the earth:

> Then another angel came out of the temple and called in a loud voice to him who was sitting on the cloud, "Take your sickle and reap, because the time to reap has come, for the harvest of the earth is ripe. So he who was seated on the cloud swung his sickle over the earth, and the earth was harvested. (Revelation 14:15–16)

An angel relays a message from God to Jesus that the time to reap the earth has come. The reaping of the earth does not sound like the pleasant experience many Christians are waiting for because Jesus (he who was seated on the cloud swung his sickle over the earth) has come for the inhabitants of the earth (and the earth was harvest). From the previous verses we could assume that the reaping of the earth will come either at the end of the reign of the RCC or it could also be at the end of the reign of Jesus. We seek an answer from the scripture that follows.

The time of harvesting will be a terrible time for those who reject Jesus:

The End of the Reign of the RCC

> The angel swung his sickle on the earth, its grapes and threw them into the great winepress of God's wrath. They were trampled in the winepress outside the city, and blood flowed out of the press, rising as high as the horses' bridles for a distance of 1,600 stadia. (Revelation 14:20)

John receives a visual of bodies trampled in a winepress outside the city with a river of flowing blood coming from it. There are a multitude of dead people who are reaped from the earth that never made it to the eternal church of Jesus Christ—they are not joining Jesus in the place of peace, they are "outside the city."

I'm a numbers guy, and there are numbers in that last verse, therefore, let's try to make sense out of it. We know that the blood is a horse's bridle high and travels 1,600 stadia. From researching the data, we find:

- 1,600 stadia is about 180 miles
- The height of a horse's bridle is about 5 feet
- A mile is 5,280 feet long
- From a visual overhead, the flow of blood should flow like a river and we are not told how wide the river of blood is
- An average person today has approximately 0.7 gallons of blood

Knowing this data, if we estimate the river at 500 feet wide, we have the following calculation to determine how much blood has been trampled out of those feeling the wrath of God:

(180 miles long x 5,280 feet/mile) x 500 feet wide x 5 feet deep x 7.481 gallons/ft3 ÷ 0.7 gallons of blood/person = 25,390,000,000 people

What can we conclude from this exercise? If we assume that the river of blood is 500 feet wide, the blood of about 25 billion people has come out of the winepress, and that's a lot of people mourning when this time comes. We can't be sure of our numbers because we had to estimate the width of the river of blood, but we can conclude that this will certainly be a period of "woe" for the inhabitants of the earth. We haven't yet decided *when* this reaping occurs; does it happen at the end of the reign of the RCC, or have we chronologically accelerated to the end of the reign of Jesus? We will address this in the next chapter.

The following quote from Jesus indicates that few see heaven, but many experience the winepress:

> Enter by the narrow gate; for wide is the gate and broad is the way that leads to destruction, and there are many who go in by it. Because narrow is the gate and difficult is the way which leads to life, and there are few who find it. (Matthew 7:13–14)

We found that there were about 25 billion inhabitants of the earth who died and were punished in the winepress, and earlier we found at the time of the end (Revelation 5:11) that those who "encircled the throne" were upon thousands in addition to 200 million. Many more find death rather than accept the gift of Jesus, just as stated in Matthew 7:13–14. I was interested

The End of the Reign of the RCC

in giving the numbers a smell test and was taken by the Spirit to https://www.prb.org/articles/how-many-people-have-ever-lived-on-earth/, where I found a table that told me the total number of people who lived between AD 1 through 1200 was estimated to be about 25.5 billion. This doesn't exactly consider our period of AD 30–1330, but it does give an indication that the numbers presented by God in prophecy are spot-on and that the reaping will occur at the end of the reign of the RCC. However, we will still look for confirmation of the timing of this event in the next chapter.

19

The Bowls of Wrath

*J*OHN OPENS REVELATION CHAPTER 15 by introducing a vision that looks marvelous to him:

> I saw in heaven another great and marvelous sign, seven angels with the seven last plagues—last because with them God's wrath is completed. (Revelation 15:1)

This is now the third sign that John is seeing in heaven since he began this chronological presentation of the church starting in chapter 12. In Revelation 12:1–2, John saw that a "great sign appeared in heaven" and we determined that this was the birth of Jesus to start the church to spread the light of the world. Then John saw another sign in heaven that was enormous, powerful, and removed some of the light of Jesus from the world (Revelation 12:3–4); Satan was out to destroy the church of Jesus Christ even before it started. This third sign seen in heaven (a great a marvelous sign) is about the family of God with him in heaven.

John receives a visual of those who received the gift of salvation from Jesus:

> And I saw what looked like a sea of glass glowing with fire and, standing beside the sea those who

had been victorious over the beast and its image and over the number of its name. They held harps given them by God and sang the song of God's servant Moses and of the Lamb. (Revelation 15:2–3)

Here we see an awesome vision in heaven with those who failed to succumb to the maddening wine of the beast and remained true to Jesus and his word (sea of class glowing with fire and, standing beside the sea those who had been victorious over the beast). Recall that when John saw the 144,000 who were the firstfruits he heard playing harps and singing loud with praises to Jesus coming from heaven. Only the 144,000 could learn the new song that would praise God and Jesus. These verses here certainly seem to represent the 144,000 who have been redeemed from the earth as opposed to the multitude who will experience the winepress and the wrath of God. We have confirmed that chapter 14 is taking place during the transition from the reign of the RCC to the reign of Jesus with his 144,000 martyrs. Earlier, John heard the 144,000 singing and playing harps of a "new song" (Revelation 14:2–3) and now John hears the song again and recognizes it as a song praising "God's servant Moses and of the Lamb."

The song of praise continues through Revelation 15:3–5, then John observes the temple of heaven:

> After this I looked, and I saw in heaven the temple—that is, the tabernacle of the covenant law—and it was opened. Out of the temple came the seven angels with the seven plagues. They were

> dressed in clean, shining linen and wore golden sashes around their chests. Then one of the four living creatures gave to the seven angels seven golden bowls filled with the wrath of God, who lives for ever and ever. And the temple was filled with smoke from the glory of God and from his power, and no one could enter the temple until the seven plagues of the seven angels were completed. (Revelation 15:5–8)

The last we heard of the ark of the covenant was when the seventh trumpet blasted ushering in the arrival of the eternal church of Jesus Christ—the ark of the covenant was seen in the temple in heaven (Revelation 11:15–19). Here we have a visual of the temple in heaven and the covenant law is exposed but the temple is empty because Jesus has left (and no one could enter the temple until the seven plagues of the seven angels were completed)! Jesus has returned to earth with the 144,000 to reign over the church, and now nobody will enter heaven until the decreed time when Jesus returns to heaven at the end of his reign in AD 2300. After the seven plagues are distributed, the wrath of God will be complete and Jesus will return to heaven to usher in the eternal church.

Jesus is reigning over the church and now the bowls of the wrath of God will be poured out on the earth:

> Then I heard a loud voice from the temple saying to the seven angels, "Go, pour out the seven bowls of God's wrath on the earth." (Revelation 16:1)

DECODING REVELATION

A loud voice from the temple of God tells the angels to start administering the wrath of God (Go, pour out the seven bowls of God's wrath) on the earth. The first bowl of wrath is poured out and there is no confusion in the message:

> The first angel went and poured out his bowl on the land, and ugly, festering sores broke out on the people who had the mark of the beast and worshiped its image. (Revelation 16:2)

It's important to note that the object of God's wrath is administered to those who worshiped the beast—the great false church (and ugly, festering sores broke out on the people who had the mark of the beast and worshiped its image). Since this bowl of wrath is dedicated to those who "had the mark of the beast and worshiped its image," we are likely early in the reign of Jesus when all Christians are members of the RCC, before John Wycliffe has interpreted the Bible for all to read. Therefore, we are looking for an event that occurred soon after AD 1330. Do we have evidence of this occurring after the reign of Jesus started in 1330 AD? Interesting enough, yes, we do.

From https://listverse.com/2017/06/25/10-factors-that-made-the-black-death-so-deadly/, we have the following:

> The plague outbreak of the mid-1300s, known widely as the Black Death because of the black, festering sores it produced on the bodies of its victims, was a terrible pandemic. It wasn't the first outbreak of the plague, but it was far and away the deadliest. Though history tends to focus on its devastation of Europe, the Black

The Bowls of Wrath

Death killed millions in a swath spanning three continents, from the British Isles to Egypt and all the way to China. Estimates of the death toll across the whole of Eurasia range from 75 to 200 million. It reduced the population of Europe by 30 to 60 percent and the population of the world as a whole from an estimated 450 million down to approximately 300–350 million between the 1340s and the mid-1350s.

The impact of the Black Death was so tremendous and destructive that it led Christians to believe they were being punished for their sins.

I hope you took note of the timing of this plague and the last sentence that stated, "It led Christians to believe they were being punished for their sins." And who were the Christians of that time called? The Catholics—the RCC. The first plague was certainly poured out by God on the beast almost immediately after Jesus left heaven to reign on earth. Do you think the beast would acknowledge that the plague was a message from God to stop their corruption of the words of Jesus? Nope—there wasn't a reaction or repentance from the beast—they just kept pushing the corruption of their church on those trying to follow Jesus just as they still do today.

God hit the beast with an "in-your-face" plague straight from the words of the book of Revelation and most experts still don't see the connection between scripture and history. Here is what the NIV states for this predicted plague:

> 16:2—*ugly, festering.* Cf. the boils and abscesses of the sixth Egyptian plague (Ex 9.9–11); see also Job 2:7–8:13)

Yah, that helped—I thought tongue in cheek. Look over here and look over there, but don't look at the beast who is staring at us in the face! Others have certainly picked up on the connection such as the site we mentioned above that stated a possible connection of this plague to the church being punished by God. However, the RCC is a very powerful force in the church that supports much of the religious machinery of profits and distribution of goods and services; and, if we connect them to the beast, this affects numerous companies, employees, and worshippers who purchase Babylon the Great goods and trinkets.

Now that the Bible is easily read, it's up to Christians to examine the rest of the plagues to see if we can correlate events to what is described in prophecy. Next, Jesus provides John a picture of the second plague:

> The second angel poured out his bowl on the sea, and it turned into blood like that of a dead person, and every living thing in the sea died. (Revelation 16:3)

You don't have to look very hard to find evidence of this plague. When Karen and I first moved to Corpus Christi we went to the beach one day to find it unusually vacated. As we walked along the beach enjoying the beautiful day and scenery, we wondered why we were the only ones on the beach enjoying it. After about five minutes, we both started getting a scratchy throat and our lungs were quickly getting irritated.

The Bowls of Wrath

We ended up abruptly leaving and when we got back home, I searched the symptoms, location, and date and quickly found a "red tide hazard warning" for our beach area.

I had never heard of the red tide before, but once you are exposed to it you will never forget it. Per https://scijinks.gov/red-tide/, we find:

> *Red tides* are sometimes also called *harmful algal blooms.* Some of the algae that causes a red tide produce powerful toxins, which are harmful chemicals that can kill fish, shellfish, mammals and birds. If people eat fish or shellfish that have been in the water with toxic algae, they will also ingest the toxins, which can make them sick.

Red tide events are known for turning the water blood red and killing everything in the sea affected by it. Thousands of dead fish wash up on shore when red tides appear, and red tides are not rare—they are very common. There were numerous red tide warnings in our years in Corpus Christi and we even experienced some during brief visits to the Gulf Coast of Florida.

Let's move on to the third plague where we also find evidence of the wrath of God being poured out as specified:

> The third angel poured out his bowl on the rivers and springs of water, and they became blood. Then I heard the angel in charge of the waters say: "You are just in these judgments, O holy One, you who are and who were; for they have shed the blood of your holy people and your prophets, and you have given them blood

to drink as they deserve." And I heard the altar respond: "Yes, Lord Almighty, true and just are your judgments." (Revelation 16:4–7)

When I searched the Internet for history that could satisfy this third plague, I found evidence that this plague might have also started. We did not find widespread evidence, but nowhere in the description of the bowls of wrath does Jesus tell us that these plagues will be complete "seven" events that affect the entire world. From the site https://www.compellingtruth.org/rivers-turning-blood-red.html, we find:

> So what is going on with blood-red water present day? Recently, credible news reports have shown water turning a blood-red color in Nootdorp, the Netherlands; Bondi Beach in Australia; the Beirut River in Lebanon; a river in Zhejiang Province, China; and even rainfall in Sewanagala, Sri Lanka.
>
> As stated above, these recent events do not line up with the chronology of end times—mainly that the tribulation has not started so neither have the trumpet or bowl judgments, nor have the two witnesses appeared. Additionally, the biblical prophecies concerning water turning to blood are enormous in scope and destruction. Also, the water in the biblical prophecies turns to blood, not just the color of blood.

The Bowls of Wrath

If you are following the reasoning of this author, you will be comforted to know that these blood-red freshwater events are not evidence of the wrath of God because the tribulation has not yet started! But wait, in our earlier analysis we found that the great tribulation (Revelation 7:14) is already past—it lasted from AD 30 to 1330, so it is already complete! Is this enough evidence? Maybe not, but there's more.

From the site https://www.online-ministries.org/sky-and-water-turning-blood-red-as-we-get-closer-to-the-great-tribulation/, comes the following:

> Rivers in China, Russia, Lebanon, and the Netherlands, as well as bodies of water in the United States, Australia, and Sri Lanka, have also turned blood red recently, as reported by reputable news outlets, leaving experts and scientists baffled. The Molchanka River in the city of Tyumen, Russia, turned red overnight, leaving locals concerned about the quality of their drinking water—and also concerned we have entered the end times.
>
> A spokesman for state watchdog Rosprirodnadzor said, "We have no assumptions as to what it could be. We have never dealt with this before so we are waiting for the results of tests." Officials in western Siberia have not yet released the results of a barrage of tests on samples taken from the river, but state-owned news agency

ITAR–TASS has labeled the incident a "biblical bombshell."

And it's not just Russia. In Nootdorp, in the Netherlands, canal water has turned a deep red, leaving locals puzzled. The phenomenon has prompted some to remember biblical prophecies of water turning to blood. "It looks like red wine," remarked Nootdorp resident Mark Ruder to the Netherlands' *Telstar Online*. "It is probably an algae," Ruder speculated, "but in our region that just does not happen."

If that isn't enough evidence and it's more blood you're looking for then what about the following example at https://www.theguardian.com/world/2019/jun/02/dday-veterans-normandy-75th-anniversary-second-world-war, where Harriet Sherwood writes an article titled, "'The sea around was red with blood, but you had to keep going': D-day veterans attend their last big gathering." I'm sure you can find many examples of dead people during the dark days of war turning the surrounding waters red with the blood of their fellow men, women, and children.

As an alternative, since the third bowl of wrath addresses the judgment of those who rejected Jesus, the second and third bowls of wrath could be the eternal death sentence for the church that is corrupt when Jesus takes reign of it. The "sea" (the church) and the "rivers and springs of water" (Jesus) are turned to blood that kills rather than blood that saves.

The Bowls of Wrath

Moving on to the fourth plague, the next few verses are very interesting:

> The fourth angel poured out his bowl on the sun, and the sun was allowed to scorch people with fire. They were seared by the intense heat and they cursed the name of God, who had control over these plagues, but they refused to repent and glorify him. (Revelation 16:8–9)

Many scientists, like me, believe that the sun is the reason for climate change and who is in the church of the sun but the Son! I also love to tell people that "I never met a government paid global warming scientist who didn't believe man was causing the earth to heat up." I didn't say there wasn't global warming, I just believe that if there is, God is responsible for it and not man.

In my humble opinion, the data is sparse and subjective, however, the winters in Michigan seem to be warmer and shorter than they were when I was a youngster. God told us that the fourth plague that will befall the planet as we get near the time of the end is the heating up of our planet. Is this happening now? Maybe, maybe not, but there is some evidence that it is. But, like specified in Revelation 16:8–9, people think they are in control of the planet's climate, and they will try to change it. Just as most people always do—once the heat becomes uncomfortable, they will "curse God" and refuse "to repent and glorify him," while they put a gaggle of ridiculous rules and regulations in place so they can fix the problem they attribute to being caused by humans. They are wasting their time—their arrogance to the Lord is the problem.

What you read above in Revelation 16:8–9 is not a concept—it is a prediction that John received from Jesus Christ about 2,000 years ago. Jesus told John it's going to get hot, so based on this scripture nobody should be surprised if the temperature of the planet increases. In summary, God is pouring out his wrath on the people of the earth who have rejected him and one of the ways we will see it is through global warming. One word of advice for all those trying to change the climate—repent and acknowledge Jesus or be prepared to fry in the heat!

We have seen evidence that the bowls of wrath are in process but are not yet complete, so we expect the same for the remaining bowls of wrath. The fifth bowl of wrath tells John that the RCC, the great false church, is the target again:

> The fifth angel poured out his bowl on the throne of the beast, and its kingdom was plunged into darkness, people gnawed their tongues in agony and cursed the God of heaven because of their pains and sores, but they refused to repent of what they had done. (Revelation 16:10–11)

This bowl of wrath is directed at the pope—the leader of the RCC (poured out his bowl on the throne of the beast). The wrath of God poured out on the pope will cause grief in the RCC. Is this a loss of membership with pain and agony for those who remain dedicated to the beast and worship it? The Internet is currently full of articles specifying turmoil in the RCC due to the actions of the current pope and maybe some of the RCC faithful have already started "gnawing their tongues in agony." The fourth bowl of wrath may be just starting, and the fifth bowl of wrath is likely just in progress or is yet to come.

There are signs that the sixth bowl of wrath may be near too:

> The sixth angel poured out his bowl on the great river Euphrates, and its water was dried up to prepare the way for the kings from the East. Then I saw three impure spirits that look like frogs; they came out of the mouth of the dragon, out of the mouth of the beast, and out of the mouth of the false prophet. They are demonic spirits that perform signs, and they go out to the kings of the whole world, to gather them for the battle on the great day of God Almighty. "Look, I come like a thief! Blessed is the one who stays awake and remains clothed, so as not to go naked and be shamefully exposed." (Revelation 16:12–15)

I found https://anfenglish.com/news/euphrates-river-is-drying-up-62209, that provided pictures of the Euphrates River drying up. This site claims:

> Latest images show that the waters of the Euphrates River have decreased significantly as a result of the water war waged by the invading Turkish state against the people of North and East Syria. Images captured on the banks of the Euphrates reveal that a large part of the Euphrates River has dried up. These areas which were

once a source of life for the region have now become arid lands. The images taken by ANHA at the Rojava Dam (Tishrin), Syria's second largest dam on the Euphrates River, show that the waters of the river have decreased significantly. The Turkish state, which has been using the Euphrates water as a weapon against the Syrians for years, cuts off the waters flowing into Iraq and Syria to a large extent.

If you do some research, you will find that some resources estimate the river Euphrates to dry up by the year 2040, but I think this is too soon. Per this bowl of wrath prophecy, once this river dries up, the devil will go on the attack by releasing "three impure spirits that look like frogs" and this is likely at or near the year AD 2330.

We learned from Daniel that the church of Jesus Christ came from the east, but here we learn that the water in the Euphrates river "was dried up to prepare the way for the kings from the East." There is only one king of the east and that is Jesus, therefore, since there is more than one king coming from the east, these must be false gods pretending to be Jesus. What will be coming out of the east as time is winding down is the devil (I saw three impure spirits that look like frogs; they came out of the mouth of the dragon) working with the remnants of the RCC (out of the mouth of the beast) together with the leader of another false religion (and out of the mouth of the false prophet) to gather for one final attack on the church of Jesus Christ to eliminate it from the earth. Jesus warns that many will die and be condemned during this time (I come like a thief!) and

The Bowls of Wrath

counsels his followers to remain dedicated to the words of Jesus (Blessed is the one who stays awake and remains clothed, so as not to go naked and be shamefully exposed").

The inhabitants of the earth will make one last stand for survival of their corrupted ways and the Lord announces that this will be the end:

> Then they gathered the kings together to the place that in Hebrew is called Armageddon. The seventh angel poured out his bowl into the air, and out of the temple came a loud voice from the throne, saying, "It is done!" (Revelation 16:16–17)

We are getting near the end now. God has had enough of the arrogance of the people that lived according to the world and says enough is enough, then hits the delete button and the world starts to end. The final plague ends up destroying the world. How does the world end? We find out in the next passages:

> Then came flashes of lightning, rumblings, peals of thunder and a severe earthquake. No earthquake like it has ever occurred since mankind has been on earth, so tremendous was the quake. (Revelation 16:18)

You have to love the clarity of the Gospel! God throws the most violent earthquake ever experienced on the earth with a qualifier—it may have been the worst earthquake ever experienced by man, but there were worse earthquakes before God created man (No earthquake like it has ever occurred since mankind *has been on the earth*). Are these nuclear bombs going off resulting in massive earthquakes? It certainly would make sense because as we see from, https://the-equivalent.com/atomic-bomb-equivalent-to-9-0-earthquake/, the detonation of a nuclear bomb could be equivalent to a 9.0 rated earthquake.

Next, John receives a damage report from the earthquake:

> The great city split into three parts, and the cities of the nations collapsed. God remembered Babylon the Great and gave her the cup filled with the wine of the fury of his wrath. (Revelation 16:19)

All those who have followed the beast and its descendants will be punished. I separated this next passage out because it has a very important message:

> Every island fled away and the mountains could not be found. (Revelation 16:20)

Remember our earlier discussion about the mountains and islands representing Jesus and the people of God? At the end as we get near the final battle that will end the earth, there is no refuge in Christ (every island fled away) because Jesus' church no longer exists (and the mountains could not be found).

As chapter 16 ends, we hear of the last bit of destruction that includes the demise of the inhabitants of the earth:

The Bowls of Wrath

> From the sky huge hailstorms, each weighting about a hundred pounds, fell on people. And they cursed God on account of the plague of hail, because the plague was so terrible. (Revelation 16:21)

I searched the Internet for the largest recorded piece of hail and found one source, https://www.severe-weather.eu/theory/hail-world-records-the-biggest-heaviest-and-deadliest-hail/ that claimed a twenty-one-pound piece of hail was recorded in Argentina. In this time when we are at the end of the world, people will be pelted with what John estimates as hail "about a hundred pounds." Are these heavy chunks of hail or are they bombs coming down from the sky? John would not know what a bomb looks like coming out of the sky, but we all know how common it is for bombs to fall from the sky. Whatever it is, the plague "was so terrible" that people cursed God for bringing this wrath down upon them. We know that the world if mostly full of nonbelievers (inhabitants of the earth), because they "cursed God on account of the plague."

The seven plagues describe the approach to the decreed time of the end. Jesus started the period of the "end times" when he gave his body as a sacrifice for the sin of all people. The church was immediately taken over by Satan who with the beasts, reigned over the church until AD 1330. Jesus returned to earth to reign with those who were martyred during the great tribulation period of the beast, then God pours out his wrath on an unrepentant people who rejected Jesus during his reign and attempted to extinguish his church. It's all about the church!

In summary, the seven plagues will not usher in the wrath of God, as we found earlier it will *complete* the pouring out of the wrath of God on those who rejected him:

- First Plague: Focused on the followers of the RCC, those who continue to worship the beast will break out in ugly festering sores.
- Second Plague: Sea water turns red and becomes contaminated.
- Third Plague: Fresh water turns red and becomes contaminated.
- Fourth Plague: Global warming scorches the earth and people cannot find solace from the extreme heat.
- Fifth Plague: The great false church, Babylon the Great, also known as "the beast" and "the RCC," will fall into darkness and their followers will refuse to repent so God will punish them and they will end up gnawing their tongues in agony.
- Sixth Plague: When the great Euphrates River dries up, three demons will be released upon the world to perform signs that persuade those following evil to gather to put an end to the church of Jesus Christ.
- Seventh Plague: Either God destroys people with a freak of nature—one-hundred-pound hailstorms or people do the job for God by bombing the world into oblivion.

The book of Revelation would be incomplete without a discussion of the fall of the church corrupted by the "inhabitants of the earth." First John receives a summary of the beast that infiltrated and destroyed the church:

The Bowls of Wrath

> One of the seven angels who had the seven bowls came and said to me, "Come, I will show you the punishment of the great prostitute, who sits by many waters. With her the kings of the earth committed adultery, and the inhabitants of the earth were intoxicated with the wine of her adulteries. (Revelation 17:1–2)

First, who is the great prostitute? We know from Revelation 12:4 and 12:14 that God took Jesus and his disciples into the wilderness to protect them for the seven of Jesus that started the church. The seed of corruption, the synagogue of Satan, was present in the church at the beginning (Revelation 2 and 3). The devil teamed with false teachers to grow and become the RCC that reigned over the church of Jesus Christ until the year AD 1330. However, we learned in Revelation 14:8 that the RCC reigned solo only until AD 1054 when there was a "Great Schism" in the church that split into two nearly indistinguishable corrupt churches that had subtle differences in their theological stew. From this we know that we had a woman representing the church, who started out as pure as Jesus, then changed over time and became *"women."* Later, Jesus referred to this great pagan church as *"Babylon the Great."* From AD 1330 until 2330, Babylon the Great does not rule, but also does not disappear. It remains a major force in the corrupt church that fragments and splits into many false churches that coexist with the church that is under the reign of Jesus and his 144,000 angels until the time of the end in AD 2330.

By the time of the end, Jesus is referring to the church as the *"great prostitute."* A *prostitute* is a woman who sells her body for immoral pleasure and wealth. In the end, the church is full of organizations that are spreading sin with a focus to make money on behalf of the name of Jesus. There is only one water of Jesus—the living water—but during the reign of Jesus, the church will have many beliefs and forms of worship (the great prostitute who sits by many waters). Many will succumb to the enticing words of the great prostitute and because they have been fooled and deceived, their names will not be written in the book of life (and the inhabitants of the earth were intoxicated with the wine of her adulteries).

The Great Prostitute, the Beast, and Death

As we entered Revelation chapter 17, we were introduced to the "great prostitute" and now we will learn how the "woman" of Revelation 12:1 evolved into this detested woman:

> Then the angel carried me away in the Spirit into a wilderness. There I saw a woman sitting on a scarlet beast that was covered with blasphemous names and had seven heads and ten horns. (Revelation 17:3)

John was last in the wilderness when the church started and was protected. Here we learn that while the church was being formed, the seed of the great prostitute, the synagogue of Satan, was already present in the church. Jesus has taken John back to the beginning of the seeds of Satan planted in the church that will corrupt it:

> The woman was dressed in purple and scarlet, and was glittering with gold, precious stones and pearls. She held a golden cup in her hand, filled with abominable things and the filth of her adul-

teries. The name written on her forehead was a mystery;

> BABYLON THE GREAT
> THE MOTHER OF PROSTITUTES
> AND THE ABOMINATIONS OF THE EARTH
>
> I saw that the woman was drunk with the blood of God's holy people; the blood of those who bore testimony to Jesus. (Revelation 17:3–6)

At the very beginning, some starting the church were focused on achieving wealth and committing sin through the church. They were very deceitful and even fooled some of the other disciples (The name written on her forehead was a mystery). All deceit in the church will grow out of these initial seeds. It started with seeds of the beast who killed Jesus (THE ABOMINATIONS OF THE EARTH), grew in power to become "BABYLON THE GREAT" during the reign of the RCC, then finally grew into many false churches during the reign of Jesus (THE MOTHER OF ALL PROSTITUTES).

As we have seen, Jesus foretold specific changes for the church:

> The beast, which you saw, once was, now is not, and yet will come up out of the Abyss and go to its destruction. The inhabitants of the earth whose names have not been written in the book of life from the creation of the world will be astonished when they see the beast, because it

once was, now is not, and yet will come. (Revelation 17:8)

The evil entity in the church will appear, then it will be removed, then it will return later. God permitted Satan to come out of the Abyss and enter the church in AD 30, then permitted Satan to attack and control the church with the help of the beast from AD 33 to 1330. In AD 1330, Jesus came down from heaven to rule with his 144,000 martyrs and threw Satan back into the Abyss for the entire thousand-year reign of Jesus (Revelation 20:2). As the thousand-year reign of Jesus ends, Satan is once again released to deceive the nations (Revelation 20:7), but the devil will be destroyed in the end (Revelation 20:10). Those who rejected Jesus to follow the beast (The inhabitants of the earth) have been decreed a permanent death (whose names have not been written in the book of life) so they will be surprised when they find out they have been fooled by the intoxicating wine of deception (will be astonished when they see the beasts).

The beast pretended he was Jesus and ruled the church and governments throughout the world (Revelation 17:9). God removed the beast's authority, but at the time of the end the beast will receive authority from the world for a brief time, then God will destroy the beast forever (Revelation 17:10-11). John receives an overall summary of the great false church throughout the future of the New Covenant:

> The ten horns you saw are ten kings who have not yet received a kingdom, but who for one

hour will receive authority as kings along with the beast. (Revelation 17:12)

The agreement between Satan and the false teachers will last the entire time of the New Covenant of Jesus (but who for one hour will receive authority as kings along with the beast). Their powerful joint attack on the church will be effective and thorough, but in the end Jesus wins:

> They have one purpose and will give their power and authority to the beast. They will wage war against the Lamb, but the lamb will triumph over them because he is Lord of lords and King of kings—and with him will be his called, chosen and faithful followers. (Revelation 17:13–14)

The RCC and their descendent faction of churches will join with Satan to hate the truth of Jesus (They will wage war against the Lamb), but ultimately Jesus will be victorious and take those who are loyal to him with him to the eternal kingdom. The RCC will remain powerful but the other factions of churches that came from her during the reign of Jesus, will hate her:

> Then the angel said to me, "The water you saw, where the prostitute sits, are peoples, multitudes, nations and languages. The beast and the ten horns you saw will hate the prostitute. They will bring her to ruin and leave her naked. (Revelation 17:15–16)

The Great Prostitute, the Beast, and Death

The RCC will split and spread their corrupt teaching throughout the world (The water you saw, where the prostitute sits, are peoples, multitudes, nations and languages). Even though all other branches of false religion are offshoots of the RCC, the RCC (the beast and the ten horns you saw) will hate all other church organizations that are offshoots of her (will hate the prostitute). For example, look at the many factions of false churches that exist today and most despise each other—especially the Catholics and vice versa.

The church will be fractured with various organizations hating each other, and the false teachers claiming to follow Jesus will be a powerful force:

> For God has put it into their hearts to accomplish his purpose by agreeing to hand over to the beast their royal authority until God's words are fulfilled. The woman you saw is the great city that rules over the kings of the earth. (Revelation 17:17–18)

God decreed the corruption in the church when he gave people free will. God permitted false teachers to corrupt the church through their free will (God has put it into their hearts to accomplish his purpose by agreeing to hand over to the beast their royal authority), but God has also decreed that it will not last forever (until God's words are fulfilled). We get verification that the initial woman that John saw in Revelation 12:1 (The woman you saw) was the church of Jesus Christ (is the great city) that rules over all the world (that rules over the kings of the earth). The church was intended to be pure from the start.

DECODING REVELATION

But we are getting close to the end:

> After I saw this I saw another angel coming down from heaven. He had great authority, and the earth was illuminated by his splendor. With a mighty voice he shouted, "Fallen! Fallen is Babylon the Great! She has become a dwelling for demons and a haunt for every impure spirit, a haunt for every unclean bird, a haunt for every unclean and detestable animal." (Revelation 18:2–3)

The pagan church (Babylon the Great) is full of evil (has become a dwelling for demons and a haunt for every impure spirit, a haunt for every unclean and detestable animal) and it will be crushed by God in due time (Fallen!). God warns people to leave behind the evil ways of the false church to follow Jesus, otherwise you will be punished:

> Then I heard another voice from heaven say: "Come out of her, my people so that you will not share in her sins, so that you will not receive any of her plagues; (Revelation 18:4)

Once the Word of God is free from the grip of Babylon the Great, people will be able to choose to follow the words of Jesus. The Lord warns all people to desert the corrupt Babylon the Great because if not, you will be physically punished (so that you will not receive any of her plagues), judged, and condemned (Revelation 18:5–8). The destruction of the false

The Great Prostitute, the Beast, and Death

churches will be swift (Therefore in one day her plagues will overtake her).

We are now getting near the end:

> When the kings of the earth who committed adultery with her and shared her luxury see the smoke of her burning, they will weep and mourn over her. Terrified at her torment, they will stand far off and cry: "Woe, woe to you, great city, you mighty city of Babylon! In one hour your doom has come!" (Revelation 18:9–10)

The end of the New Covenant has arrived because the Lord says, "In one hour your doom has come!" God decreed the 2,300 years as the hour of the New Covenant, but the time will come when the hour is up. John receives more details about what happens when the great false church is removed from the earth:

> "Every sea captain, and all who travel by ship, the sailors, and all who earn their living from the sea, will stand far off. When they see the smoke of her burning, they will exclaim, 'Was there ever a city like this great city?'" (Revelation 18:17–18)

Every church leader (sea captain), their followers (and all who traveled by ship, the sailors), and even the merchants who have benefited from peddling the trinkets sold for churches and those who work for the church (and all who earn their living from the sea) will be saddened when Babylon the Great is destroyed.

Then, in an instant, the woman posing as the church of Jesus Christ will be destroyed:

> Then a mighty angel picked up a boulder the size of a large millstone and threw it into the sea, and said, "With such violence the great city of Babylon will be thrown down never to be found again." (Revelation 18:21)

Jesus selected the word *"millstone"* to represent the death of the great false church because a millstone is used to grind wheat or grain—it is used to prepare food. If you recall, the third seal revealed that the RCC changed the Word of God to a message that starved people of the spiritual food of Jesus. The church became an institution benefiting from feeding people garbage rather than the words of life, and God who prepared the true food, destroys the church in the end with a message addressing the garbage they tried to pass off as spiritual food. Jesus emphasized the importance of this word in the following caution:

> Whoever will cause one of these little ones who believe in me to stumble, it would be better for him if he were thrown into the sea with a millstone hung around his neck. (Mark 9:42)

If you are a preacher or teacher of the world trying to program children to follow your evil ways, you will be severely punished in the end. The Lord knows what you are doing and

The Great Prostitute, the Beast, and Death

warns you in advance to turn from your evil ways to follow the words of Jesus.

The souls in heaven rejoice that God finally removed the stain of the beast from the earth:

> After this I heard what sounded like the roar of a great multitude in heaven shouting: "Hallelujah! Salvation and glory and power belong to our God, for true and just are his judgments. He has condemned the great prostitute who corrupted the earth by her adulteries. He has avenged on her the blood of his servants." (Revelation 19:1–2)

Those in heaven rejoice with the death of Satan and the beast who posed as the church. John says that it is "the roar of a great multitude in heaven." Heaven must be open for business again when the great false church is destroyed; we know that Jesus is back in heaven because it is time for judgment (Salvation and glory and power belong to our God, for true and just are his judgments). Those who corrupted the church are held accountable (He has condemned the great prostitute who corrupted the earth by her adulteries) and the followers of Jesus who were executed will finally have their promised vengeance (He has avenged on her the blood of his servants).

The great multitude praises God:

> Then I heard what sounded like a great multitude, like the roar of rushing waters and like loud peals of thunder shouting: "Hallelujah! For our Lord God Almighty reigns." (Revelation 19:6)

DECODING REVELATION

There is a great number of people waiting for the return of Jesus to heaven (Then I heard what sounded like a great multitude). Jesus is the living water and the multitude of people who have been saved through the blood of Jesus are anxiously waiting for his return. Heaven has been closed, so at the time of the end, all those saved through the blood of Jesus except for the 144,000 who have already been resurrected, will be drawn to heaven to be with Jesus (like the roar of rushing waters and like loud peals of thunder shouting: Hallelujah!) because Jesus rules (For our Lord God Almighty reigns).

Those who have been saved by the blood of Jesus are ready for the wedding feast of the Lamb:

> Let us rejoice and be glad and give him glory! For the wedding of the Lamb has come, and his bride has made herself ready. Fine linen, bright and clean was given her to wear. (Fine linen stands for the righteous acts of God's holy people.) (Revelation 19:7–8)

Then, there is a transition verse:

> Then the angel said to me, "Write this: Blessed are those who are invited to the wedding supper of the Lamb!" (Revelation 19:9)

And who will be invited to the wedding supper of the Lamb? All those who follow Jesus. John is initially overwhelmed, so the servant of Jesus delivering the message helps John to grasp what he is being told:

The Great Prostitute, the Beast, and Death

> At this I fell at his feet to worship him. But he said to me, "Don't do that! I am a fellow servant with you and with your brothers and sisters who hold to the testimony of Jesus. Worship God! For it is the Spirit of prophecy who bears testimony to Jesus." (Revelation 19:10–11)

John fell down to worship the servant of Jesus and is bluntly told that the only one who John or anyone is to worship is God and his Son Jesus who is being described in this prophecy. Everyone who worships God must pay attention to prophecy to ensure they are worshiping Jesus and not just a "fellow servant."

Next, Revelation 19:12–13 presents a visual of Jesus then John receives a recap of why we praise only Jesus:

> The armies of heaven were following him, riding on white horses and dressed in fine linen, white and clean. Coming out of his mouth is a sharp sword with which to strike down the nations. He will rule them with an iron scepter. He treads the winepress of the fury of the wrath of God Almighty. (Revelation 19:14–15)

John will get a summary of the church from the beginning until the coming of the Lord with the eternal church—the reason why it's important to praise Jesus. The servant describes Jesus' arrival on earth to bring salvation to the world (Revelation 6:2). We know that Jesus' rule and reign is decreed and should not be challenged, but the synagogue of Satan took over the church and, in the end, they paid the price for it (he treads the winepress of the fury of the wrath of God Almighty). Only Jesus is to be worshiped in the church and nothing else:

> On his robe and on his thigh he has this name written: KING OF KINGS AND LORD OF LORDS. (Revelation 19:16)

But that isn't what happened—the RCC took over the church and the wrath of God came upon them:

> And I saw an angel standing in the sun, who cried in a loud voice to all the birds flying in midair, "Come, gather together for the great supper of God, so that you may eat the flesh of kings, generals, and the mighty, of horses and their riders, and the flesh of all people, free and slave, great and small. (Revelation 19:17–18)

We return to the winepress that resulted in the eternal death of those who took over the church. Jesus returned to the earth at the end of the reign of the RCC and all the inhabitants of the earth who rejected Jesus and followed the beast were harvested.

It was not an easy journey for Jesus to come and reign over the church—the RCC did not go down without a fight:

> Then I saw the beast and the kings of the earth and their armies gathered together to wage war against the rider on the horse and his army. But the beast was captured, and with it the false prophet who had performed the signs on its behalf. With these signs he had deluded those who

The Great Prostitute, the Beast, and Death

had received the mark of the beast and worshiped its image. The two of them were thrown alive into the fiery lake of burning sulfur. The rest were killed with the sword coming out of the mouth of the rider on the horse, and all the birds gorged themselves on their flesh. (Revelation 19:19–21)

Satan and the RCC and their pope fought to maintain control over the church, but Jesus won, and the pope lost the total control it had on people in the church. The devil who was in control no longer had free reign over the church with the leader of the RCC—the pope (and with it the false prophet who had performed the signs on its behalf) who fooled many people trying to follow Jesus (With these signs he had deluded those who had received the mark of the beast and worshiped its image). The devil and the pope who are working together, are punished (The two of them were thrown alive into the fiery lake of burning sulfur) and those following this evil duo are condemned to eternal death (were killed with the sword coming out of the mouth of the rider on the horse—the winepress (Revelation 14:18–20).

The Transition to Jesus—Heaven Is Silent

REMEMBER WHEN WE EXAMINED the seals and found that one short verse, Revelation 8:1, described the entire thousand-year reign of Jesus that followed the reign of the beast? In summary, we were presented the following progression of events in chapter 19:

- Revelation 19:9—The wedding supper of the Lamb—the eternal church of Jesus Christ will come at the time of the end.
- Revelation 19:10–11—Only those who worship Jesus, and only Jesus, will get an invitation.
- Revelation 19:12–15—The invitation comes from the church that Jesus leads, and he will punish those who corrupt it.
- Revelation 19:16—The worship of Jesus is the only reason for the church to exists.
- Revelation 19:17–18—Jesus owns the church but men who had power on earth believed that they had the power of God, took the church from the followers of Jesus.
- Revelation 19:19–21—The evil false teachers took over the church by force, but the Lord ended their control over the church when he locked up the RCC and their

pope to prevent them from controlling the church anymore and he punished those who followed the beast.

At the end of chapter 19 of Revelation the church was in transition. Chapter 20 of Revelation starts out providing John the details of this transition:

> And I saw an angel coming down out of heaven, having the key to the Abyss and holding in his hand a great chain. He seized the dragon, that ancient serpent, who is the devil, or Satan, and bound him for a thousand years. He threw him into the Abyss, and locked and sealed it over him, to keep him from deceiving the nations anymore until the thousand years were ended. After that, he must be set free for a short time. (Revelation 20:1–3)

We saw at the end of chapter 19 how the beast—the pope—was contained and punished, and the followers of the beast met their doom, but we have yet to learn how all this was accomplished. The Lord snatched Satan from the world and locked him up while Jesus is reigning over the church. Many see this thousand-year reign of Jesus as coming in the distant future. However, put into context with the ending of chapter 19 of Revelation and combined with the prophecy of Daniel for the time of the end (Daniel 8:14) we find that it came right after the end of the reign of the RCC. When combined with the following verses, we can be assured that we are addressing the transition that has already occurred.

The Transition to Jesus—Heaven Is Silent

The next verse tells the church that there are two phases of resurrection and judgment:

> I saw thrones on which were seated those who had been given authority to judge. And I saw the souls of those who had been beheaded because of their testimony about Jesus and because of the word of God. They had not worshiped the beast or its image and had not received its mark on their foreheads or their hands. They came to life and reigned with Christ a thousand years. (The rest of the dead did not come to life until the thousand years were ended.) This is the first resurrection. (Revelation 20:4–5)

The transition is a time of judgment (I saw thrones on which were seated those who had been given authority to judge), vengeance for those who were killed during the great tribulation (And I saw the souls of those who had been beheaded because of their testimony about Jesus and because of the word of God), and resurrection of those who were martyred during the reign of the beast (They came to life and reigned with Christ). The 144,000 who were executed by the RCC throughout the period of their reign from AD 33 to 1330, will be resurrected to reign over the church with Jesus. This passage verifies that the 144,000 firstfruits from Revelation 14:4, were resurrected to reign with Jesus in what has been called the "first resurrection." There are others that were saved during the reign of the beast, but they will not be resurrected with the Lord until the end of the thousand-year reign of Jesus (The rest of the dead did not come to life until the thousand years were ended.). How do we know they are followers of Jesus? Because they "come to life" after the thousand-year reign of Jesus ends.

If you ignore the beast and what happens to the church, you can present other conclusions and interpretations and although they don't make sense, I can understand why theologians and preachers avoid the intended discussion of the beast—it's not an easy and welcome subject. Can you imagine preachers in every church calling out other organizations of Christians for following Satan? It's not a pleasant thought but, as we are getting near the end of our analysis of Revelation, this is clearly what Jesus wants. In the future, anyone who fails to completely address the beast when preaching Daniel or Revelation is doing a disservice to their assembly.

Using www.biblegateway.com, I searched the NIV interpretation of the Bible to find the number of references to *"beast"* and found the following:

- The Bible has eighty-seven references to the beast—fifty-one in the Old Testament and thirty-six in the New Testament.
- Daniel has the most references to the beast of any Old Testament book—eleven in total.
- Revelation contains thirty-four of the New Testament references to the beast.
- Together, Daniel and Revelation contain forty-five of the eighty-seven references to the beast—a whopping 52%, or just over half of the total.

The Transition to Jesus—Heaven Is Silent

With these bullets as a starting point, can any sermon or message on Daniel *and* Revelation avoid a full and thorough discussion of the beast? I wouldn't think so, but in general the elders of the church and followers of Jesus ignore the beast. I searched the Internet for *"the book of Revelation explained"* and *"the book of Daniel explained"* and the first page of the first three websites for each that I looked at ignored the beast. The beast is one of the most important topics of prophecy in Revelation and Daniel yet the church ignores it! But why?

When it comes to the beast, the church has two options—recognize it as present in the church and address it or point to some unknown scary beast in the future. It's easier to point to the future rather than digging through the details of prophecy to try to identify a beast within the church. Looking for a beast in the church is a very unpleasant prospect and undertaking. If the beast is brought up, people might be turned off from the church and the objective is to get as many people into the church as possible—even if the assembly must water down scripture and allow sin in the church. Many sermons inform church attendees about sin in the church, but I've yet to hear a preacher point to the beast and explain its presence in the church; they would rather welcome and continue to teach theological stew that points to a future beast. The beast prophesied in both Daniel and Revelation was decreed and it arrived on time and greatly affected the church during the hour of Jesus. It remains in the church and is prominent throughout. It was prophesied and it has been fulfilled. The church does Jesus a disservice by ignoring its presence throughout the church.

Moving on in chapter 20, those who reign with Jesus are blessed like the disciples were stated to have been blessed for

being with Jesus during his mission, watching him crucified and rise from the dead, then starting the church (Daniel 12:12):

> Blessed and holy are those who share in the first resurrection. The second death has no power over them, but they will be priests of God and of Christ and will reign with him for a thousand years. (Revelation 20:6)

The 144,000 martyrs are still reigning with Jesus over the church as "priests of God and of Christ." The martyrs are like angels who assist the church to fight evil and stay true to worshiping only Jesus. If you have done the math, you are certainly aware by now that we are currently at the tail end of this thousand-year reign of Jesus that started in AD 1330—it is winding down as there is about 300 years remaining. We are also running out of chapters in the book of Revelation, so it's time to get an understanding of what will happen when the thousand-year reign of Jesus ends in AD 2330:

> When the thousand years are over, Satan will be released from his prison and will go out to deceive the nations in the four corners of the earth—Gog and Magog—and to gather them for battle. In number they are like the sand on the seashore. They marched across the breadth of the earth and surrounded the camp of God's people, the city he loves. But fire came down from heaven and devoured them. (Revelation 20:7–9)

The Transition to Jesus—Heaven Is Silent

The thousand-year reign of Jesus ends with the church being reconsecrated in AD 2330 (see Daniel 8:14 and the analysis of that verse in *Unraveling Daniel*). The reign of Jesus has had a good run, but that ripe period for converting people to follow Jesus is rapidly coming to an end. We can see all around us that the church attacks are picking up and the youth are rejecting Jesus and his church.

In the three verses above we see that in AD 2330 there will be one final push by Satan and his minions to destroy the church. Note that in AD 2330 the inhabitants of the earth completely cover the earth—their numbers "are like the sand on the seashore." Alternatively, the church is nearly extinct—it is considered a "camp of God's people," but even though there are only a few followers of Jesus left, they are told that God loves them (God's people, the city he loves). Then the remaining few in the church together with the numerous inhabitants of the earth are destroyed by something that seems like a barrage of missiles or a meteor (But fire came down from heaven and devoured them).

I know you are wondering what *"Gog"* and *"Magog"* are because so was I. An interesting thing happened as I typed up that previous paragraph; when I typed *"Gog"* I accidentally typed *"God"* because it is so similar. After that, I considered that Gog might not be a real place—it just signifies that God will no longer be present on the earth. The church is quickly approaching a time when there will be no more church left—the world will be *"Gog and Magog"*—a replacement for "God" and "My God."

However, the ending has a silver lining:

> And the devil, who deceived them, was thrown into the lake of burning sulfur, where the beast and the false prophet had been thrown. They will be tormented day and night for ever and ever. (Revelation 20:10)

At the end of the thousand years, the devil will be thrown into hell, where God threw the RCC and the false prophet that worked together to deceive the nations. The wrath of God will end up killing everyone who is left on the earth, then there is only one thing left—judgment.

22

Judgment and Rewards

*T*HE REMAINING SMALL GROUP of followers of Jesus are killed, then there is only one thing left—judgment for those who rejected Jesus and persecuted the church. As we presented earlier in John 5:24, contrary to popular belief, those who follow Jesus will not face judgment. This is not the case for those who rejected Jesus:

> He who rejects me, and doesn't receive my sayings, has one who judges him. The word that I spoke will judge him in the last day. (John 12:48)

Those who reject Jesus have a very simple judgment—God condemns them for their disbelief.

But there is another judgment:

> Then I saw a great white throne and him who was seated on it. The earth and the heavens fled from his presence, and there was no place for them. And I saw the dead, great and small, standing before the throne, and books were opened. Another book was opened, which is the book of life. The dead were judged according to what they had done as recorded in the books. The sea gave up the dead that were in it, and death and Hades gave up the dead that were in them, and

each person was judged according to what they had done. (Revelation 20:11–13)

There is a transition coming because *both* "the earth and the heavens fled from his presence"—God is on his throne and heaven and earth are no longer in existence. It's time for Jesus to judge the dead—both those who followed God (great) and those who rejected God (and small). We know from scripture that there is one book of life with names written in it, but here we learn of multiple books being opened (and *books* were opened). These books are not the book of life—they are different, and we find out why they are different from Revelation 20:13—they contain the deeds of people (each person was judged according to what they had done).

If you've ever wondered about what happens to people who never heard of Jesus or who have been fooled by the words of false teachers, you have just been told that they will be judged by their actions. If their actions followed the words of Jesus presented by the true church (The sea gave up the dead that were in it) they are redeemed and saved. However, if their actions proved that they followed Satan and evil, they are condemned (and death and Hades gave up the dead that were in them). Remember the pale horse that stated the riders name was death, and "Hades was following close behind" (Revelation 6:8)? Hell is following close behind those who died after rejecting God.

We get confirmation of this concept in the following verses of scripture:

Judgment and Rewards

> Don't marvel at this, for the hour comes, in which all that are in the tombs will hear his voice, and will come out; those who have done good, to the resurrection of life; and those who have done evil, to the resurrection of judgment. (John 5:28–29)

> I tell you that every idle word that men speak, they will give account of it in the day of judgment. For by your words you will be justified, and by your words you will be condemned." (Matthew 12:36–37)

> For the Son of Man will come in the glory of his Father with his angels, and then he will render to everyone according to his deeds. (Matthew 16:27)

In the end, everyone will hear the voice of Jesus and be saved or condemned. If you've never heard of Jesus but you lived as though you did and try to follow him, your deeds will confirm this. If you followed evil, your deeds will confirm this too. If you stated you followed Jesus, but your deeds prove that you followed evil, Jesus knows the truth and you will also be condemned.

We then read about the judgment that will take place from the book of life:

> Then death and Hades were thrown into the lake of fire. The lake of fire is the second death. Anyone whose name was not found written in

the book of life was thrown into the lake of fire. (Revelation 20:14–15)

Those who rejected God are thrown into the lake of fire. Those who followed the words of Jesus and their deeds proved it, have their names written in the book of life and will be saved. There is the multitude from the church who followed the words of Jesus that will bypass judgment, hear the voice of Jesus at the time of the end, and be called home to spend eternity with Jesus:

> He who believes in him is not judged. He who doesn't believe has been judged already, because he has not believed in the name of the one and only Son of God. (John 3:18)

> "Most certainly I tell you, he who hears my word and believes him who sent me has eternal life, and doesn't come into judgment, but has passed out of death into life. (John 5:24)

> This is the will of my Father who sent me, that of all he has given to me I should lose nothing, but should raise them up at the last day. This is the will of the one who sent me, that everyone who sees the Son, and believes in him, should have eternal life; and I will raise him up at the last day." (John 6:39–40)

> "But I don't seek my own glory. There is one who seeks and judges. Most certainly, I tell you, if a

Judgment and Rewards

person keeps my word, he will never see death."
(John 8:50–51)

According to Revelation 20:15, reject Jesus and you are thrown into the lake of fire. There is no question and no debating—reject Jesus and you go to hell. Accept Jesus and you go to heaven. Pretend you believe in Jesus, and you also go to hell—you are not a follower of Jesus.

Then John receives a visual of the reward waiting for the followers of Jesus:

> Then I saw "a new heaven and a new earth," for the first heaven and first earth had passed away, and there was no longer any sea. I saw the Holy City, the new Jerusalem, coming down out of heaven from God, prepared as a bride beautifully dressed for her husband. And I heard a loud voice from the throne saying, "Look! God's dwelling place is now among the people, and he will dwell with them. They will be his people, and God himself will be with them and be their God. (Revelation 21:1–3)

The former earth and heaven no longer exist—the church on earth is gone! Jesus is informing the disciple John about what comes after the end of the world for those who are saved. The earth as we know it will end and our existence in the rebuilt heaven is assured (Then I saw "a new heaven and a new earth," for the first heaven and first earth had passed away). There is no need for the Word of God or the church in the new existence (and there was no longer any sea) and that seems a bit strange, so why is that? Because in eternity, we will always be in the presence of the Lord; the church, Jesus, earth, and heaven have all become one (I saw the Holy City, the new Jerusalem, coming down out of heaven from God, prepared as a bride beautifully dressed for her husband). God is no longer on the throne in some distant place called *"heaven,"* we are with God for eternity (God's dwelling place is now among the people, and he will dwell with them). We will be forever with God praising him in the New Jerusalem.

These next few passages summarize the message of Jesus completely and beautifully:

> He said to me, "It is done. I am the Alpha and the Omega, the Beginning and the End. To the thirsty I will give water without cost from the spring of the water of life. Those who are victorious will inherit all this, and I will be their God and they will be my children. But the cowardly, the unbelieving, the vile, the murderers, the sexually immoral, those who practice magic arts, the idolaters and all liars—they will be consigned to the fiery lake of burning sulfur. This is the second death. (Revelation 21:6–8)

Those who follow the Word of God will be victorious and inherit the kingdom of God. However—and that's a big however—Jesus provides a long list of those who live according to the ways of the world to pleasure their flesh who will not share in the reward (cowardly, the unbelieving, the vile, the murderers, the sexually immoral, those who practice magic arts,

Judgment and Rewards

the idolaters and all liars). Those who follow evil will be condemned to an everlasting torturous death. I hope you paid close attention to that long list of those who will suffer for eternity in the second death—I did! In fact, this summary is so important, the list of those who will experience the second death is repeated in verse 22:15 toward the end of this prophetic book. We all fall into that list at some time in our lives—some spend their entire life living that list. The warning is to remind us that we *all* are sinners who separate ourselves from God and there is no way to bridge this divide other than through the acceptance of the sacrifice of his Son, Jesus.

The church and Jesus were pure at the very beginning and now at the end, Jesus and his people become united in purity:

> One of the seven angels who had the seven bowls full of the seven last plagues came and said to me, "Come, I will show you the bride, the wife of the Lamb." (Revelation 21:9)

Just as a bride and groom are two and separate then become united as one, Jesus and his creation of people will be united and become one together for eternity (I will show you the bride, the wife of the Lamb). The wedding between Jesus and his creation commences:

> And he carried me away in the spirit to a mountain great and high, and showed me the Holy City, Jerusalem, coming down out of heaven from God. (Revelation 21:10)

 DECODING REVELATION

It's as though we have just received an introduction; Heaven meet earth . . . earth meet heaven. There are no longer two entities of heaven and earth—they are now one! Of course, the union is formalized on a mountain just as the law was presented and the twelve disciples of Jesus were selected on mountains. Jesus as the Holy City, Jerusalem, makes his presence known in the new heaven and earth (the Holy City, Jerusalem, coming down out of heaven from God). Verses 21:11–22:5 describe the eternal paradise that is waiting for those who are worthy. Afterward, Jesus provides John a summary of what John has seen:

> The angel said to me, "These words are trustworthy and true. The Lord, the God who inspires the prophets, sent his angel to show his servants the things that must soon take place. (Revelation 22:6)

I hope you picked up on the word *"servants"* because this is very important. Jesus provided this revelation to John, "He made it known by sending his angel to his servant John" (Revelation 1:1). John is not to keep this revelation to himself; he is to share it with *all* the "servants" of Jesus (sent his angel to show his servants). In summary, John has been shown "what must soon take place," and we now know that *"soon"* meant through the year AD 2330; then, the world will transition to the eternal kingdom. The words we have presented and analyzed from the book of Revelation are the words of Jesus through an angel. God gave prophets his word to document, and God also gave his angels to share visions with his servants to provide

Judgment and Rewards

special messages. Messages don't get any more special than the one provided to John documented in Revelation.

The end is coming soon for us all:

> "Look, I am coming soon! Blessed is the one who keeps the words of the prophecy written in this scroll." (Revelation 22:7)

Jesus tells you that you are blessed if you "keep" the words of the prophecy written in this scroll. Keeping these words of prophecy can only be achieved through *understanding* and *living* them. Jesus' message contained in Revelation was always intended to be a *clear* message without any confusion. The book of Revelation was meant to be understood and obeyed by all—it was not provided with the confused meaning presented by preachers and teachers. A person will unravel Revelation by knowing it is all about the church of Jesus Christ *and* evil will try to destroy them both. Take away either portion of that message and Revelation becomes a mystery. Remove Jesus, his church, and/or the beast from every aspect of Revelation and you are confused. The Lord wants you to believe in Jesus and *know and understand the hazards* you face to do this.

Jesus understands that people resist change:

> Let the one who does wrong continue to do wrong; let the vile person continue to be vile; let the one who does right continue to do right; and let the holy person continue to be holy." Look, I am coming soon! My reward is with me, and I will give to each person according to what they have done. (Revelation 22:11–12)

DECODING REVELATION

Jesus knows that people are on a path and it's difficult for them to change—even with the words of caution about eternal death that he has provided. Everyone is leaving this earth soon, but the future is not uncertain—you will be with Jesus in eternity if you follow him. The prophecy in this book is meant to help you see the light and avoid the second and permanent death.

The Holy Spirit continued to provide me a path forward when, on the same day I submitted the book *Unraveling Daniel* to the publisher, I received the following vision:

> May 11, 2023—You are to contact all preachers and teachers to let them know that they are not to present another sermon of Daniel and Revelation until they read the book you just submitted for publication—*Unraveling Daniel.*

How's that for direction? I woke up and couldn't go back to sleep because this vision troubled me. How am I supposed to contact *all* preachers and teachers to let them know the correct interpretation of Daniel and Revelation so that they change their theology to expose the beast? My first two books that led to *Unraveling Daniel* and *Decoding Revelation* have thus far been rejected by every preacher and teacher I have approached. At first, I struggled with finding a way to fulfill the vision's command, but with further guidance from the Holy Spirit, the book cover and preface for *Unraveling Daniel* addressed this vision by sharing the message to "read, understand, and share this truth." I continue to pray for direction, guidance, and strength to fulfill my commitment to follow wherever the Lord leads.

The Warning

As I was getting to the end of our analysis of Daniel and Revelation prophecy, I was considering what the closing message will be. I hadn't heard from the Lord yet on how to wrap up this book, then I read the verses at the end, and I knew what the ending had to be. The closing verses near the end of the book of Revelation have a very important verse that I didn't completely understand until the final iteration. Only after numerous reviews of the message did I grasp the meaning of the following:

> I warn everyone who hears the words of the prophecy of this scroll: If anyone adds anything to them, God will add to that person the plagues described in this scroll. And if anyone takes words away from this scroll of prophecy, God will take away from that person any share in the tree of life and in the Holy City, which are described in this scroll. (Revelation 22:18–19)

I have often wondered if these verses addressed the book of Revelation or *all scripture*. I don't wonder any more. Anyone "who *hears* the words of the prophecy" has certainly read other sections of the Bible and is studying the words of Jesus. Therefore, the message above is written to everyone in the

DECODING REVELATION

church, and they are warned to keep from adding words to this prophecy. Think about that and consider what you hear when you are listening to a sermon about prophecy. Is John being sentenced to a prison in Patmos as an old man in this scripture? Nope! Is the seven-year tribulation period with an antichrist mentioned in this scripture? Nope! The false teachers didn't *physically* add words to John's vision recorded in Revelation, they twisted the meaning of it through *creating and spreading tradition*—just like these same false teachers have twisted the words of scripture through tradition to claim that Matthew, Mark, and Luke were Gospel authors.

Note that the warning is specific about removing "words" from prophecy, but it does not mention specifically adding "words" to it—it says, "adds anything." Jesus is clearly warning the church that false teachers will change the meaning of the scroll by *adding tradition* to the prophecy. *The Early Church Father Catholic Fraud* provided details of how the false teachers twisted the meaning of scripture to validate the existence of the beast through tradition that claimed Matthew, Mark, and Luke wrote Gospels. We proved that this was not the truth. The ending of Revelation is a warning to you that false teachers will use tradition to change the meaning of prophecy to point you away from them—the beast. Their plan has worked for many years, but the time has come to expose it and eliminate them and tradition from the church. Just as with the prophecy in Daniel that we clarified in *Unraveling Daniel,* all future sermons and teaching about Revelation prophecy is now required to address the beast that has now been exposed history that proves prophecy.

Jesus had John write these words at the end of this prophetic book because he knew what was going to happen. Jesus knew

The Warning

that the RCC would claim Peter lives through their leader, the pope (Revelation 13:3 and 13:12) and they would take over the church. That alone should have you believing the rest of the story presented in Revelation. Think about that for another minute—Jesus predicted that the RCC would bring Peter to life in the form of their false church and assign a leader to rule over the church. Jesus also told us how the great false church would grow and spread out to become the "great prostitute." How much more detailed and precise can God be? Jesus knew that false teachers would corrupt the church then try and hide their deception. How much of the tradition being repeated as truth in churches can be believed? I return to 1 John 2:18–19 and claim that none of it can be believed. The RCC did their best to scrub church documentation to ensure that there was a story of Peter as the leader of the church that could be believed. It has been believed by a multitude who still—even when exposed to the truth—pledge their allegiance to this great false church. The RCC did their best to cover their crime, but God gave us prophecy with the hidden details presented in a puzzle to expose the corruption of false teachers. Just like God left the breadcrumbs to determine the names of those who wrote the Gospels, God left breadcrumbs in prophecy that would one day be put together to reveal the level of corruption in the church.

Like we presented earlier, warning about the beast is one of the main themes of prophecy, and we have exposed the beast. What has been prophesied about the beast and its' effect on the free church have been proven through history to be accurate predictions. With the RCC's introduction of tradition and the teaching of it throughout the church, the RCC corrupted *the entire* church. Jesus knew that people would add interpretations

DECODING REVELATION

and words of tradition to the prophecy in the book to give it a meaning other than what was intended. As we already mentioned, prophecy is about Jesus and his church and unfortunately it is also a story about how the church will be affected by corruption. Corruption in the church kept me from being a believer in Jesus for many years, and now that the Lord has been gracious enough to allow me to address my doubts and expose the truth, I'm eager to share it.

If you recall, I had two visions on April 21, 2022, that I described earlier in this book. The first vision told me that the church was dirty and I needed to clean it up. The second vision that morning proved to me and my wife Karen that the Holy Spirit was actively working within me to expose the dirty church and provide the data that will help the church clean up their act. I just recently reached out to an individual who the Lord told me was turning his back on the Lord and will be called home soon. This individual snubbed God again just as he had done in the past. In addition, to try to get the word out about the corruption in the church, I have joined four "Christian" forums to engage with others. In each case I have been kicked out and banned from participation for telling the truth. Most so-called Christians do not want to hear the truth—they want a Jesus that fits their lifestyle and supports the type of church they have connected to regardless of whether they follow scripture. Expose or talk about a beast and you are unwelcome. However, this is not what the Holy Spirit is telling me.

I received a vision that I wrote down in November 2022 that provided a great summary for the ending of this book:

The Warning

This morning I woke up very early at 12 a.m. after about three hours of sleep with the following vision. I was at my father's house, and it was peaceful. A wind started blowing and it kept picking up speed and soon became violent and ferocious. The house started shaking and soon it started slowly moving. The house kept moving as it shook, and I hoped it was not going to fall off its foundation. The house kept moving and picking up speed, until pieces of the house started dislodging and the house started to head down a slope. The slope kept increasing as we headed downward then suddenly, the house hit the end of the hill and fell off a cliff with the house crumbling into pieces. As I was falling I prayed hard to Jesus to take me into paradise as we continued in the free fall—then it ended.

As I laid there in bed wondering the meaning of the vision, I asked, "Lord, are you letting me know that your house was attacked and fell apart, for I have now seen these things?" The Lord has shown me how the church started out pure, but that purity lasted for only the instant that Jesus committed his sacrifice for our salvation. As soon as the sacrifice was made, the church of Jesus Christ was attacked. It was initially protected to give it a solid footing, otherwise Satan together with those choosing to follow evil would have destroyed it. Since then, the church has been attacked and controlled by the beast. Even when Jesus returned to rule over it with martyrs who were killed for their faith, the attacks didn't stop.

DECODING REVELATION

We have a church that is crumbling away with a growing contempt for the words of Jesus. The elders of the church neither confront the beast nor attempt to remove it from the church. The church is corrupt through and through and most people who call themselves Christians are pretenders. As I have stated, four out of four Christian forums banned me for attempting to expose the beast as I have been instructed to do. The elders of the churches I attend don't want to hear about the corruption in the church and neither do most who call themselves Christians. The church that is composed of Mormons, Catholics, Methodists, Lutherans, and hundreds of other factions of the church with various names are sticking to their tradition and ignoring scripture, and this welcomes the beast that struts throughout the church.

Elders—you are to teach only scripture and eliminate tradition from the church, because tradition is causing the church to crumble. Christians—don't accept attending a church that is crumbling under a corrupted message as described in the first four seals. You have access to a Bible and are responsible for ensuring the message you receive from your church is from Jesus. You have been told what will happen to you if you ignore the words of Jesus, so take heed!

Paul refers to our bodies as *"tents"* because they are temporary housing:

> For we know that if the earthly house of our tent is dissolved, we have a building from God, a house not made with hands, eternal, in the heavens. (2 Corinthians 5:1)

The Warning

Our bodies are crumbling but we are to lean upon the church to strengthen us. Ensure that your church is built upon the strength of Jesus and, therefore, is not crumbling into pieces as you approach the collapse of your tent. I'm going to end this book with a prayer for you to commit to making the changes in your life that will bring you closer to Jesus:

> Lord, Father in Heaven, I start out this prayer with praise and worship of you and your Son, Jesus, and I thank you for all you have done in my life. I recognize that I am a sinner in need of cleansing, and I ask for the forgiveness of my sin through the belief in your Son, Jesus. I repent of my sin and will use this opportunity to promise to read and try to understand only your word. I seek your directions and guidance for my life. In Jesus' name I pray.

If you have said this prayer, I recommend you find a church that preaches Jesus from scripture and does not add to or delete from the apostle's documentation. Avoid discussions of tradition because it is not the Word of God—it is hidden and deceitful corruption trying to steal the Word of God from you. Heed the warnings of Jesus as he ended Revelation, not to add or delete anything from prophecy. If you do this, you will ensure the house of God you attend is on a solid foundation and will not fall down that cliff and crumble as it tumbles off the mountain.

www.ingramcontent.com/pod-product-compliance
Lightning Source LLC
Chambersburg PA
CBHW031309150426
43191CB00005B/152